Talking Acadian

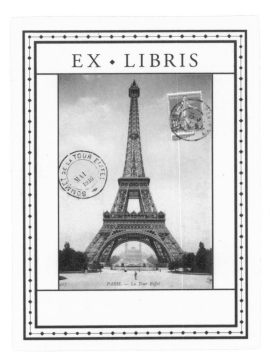

EX · LIBRIS

PARIS. — La Tour Eiffel

Talking Acadian
Communication, Work, and Culture

John Chetro-Szivos
CHAIR, DEPARTMENT OF COMMUNICATION
Fitchburg State College, MA

YBK Publishers, Inc.
New York

Chetro-Szivos: *Talking Acadian: Communication, Work, and Culture*

Copyright © 2006 by John Chetro-Szivos

YBK Publishers, Inc.
39 Crosby St.
New York, NY 10013

ISBN 0-9764359-6-9

Library of Congress Control Number: 2006931435

Manufactured in the United States of America

Ver 06-08

To my wife Annette and my beautiful American children Erika and Kiel:

You are the beautiful dreams of immigrants before you:
tapestries of words, hopes, and love.
Carry the dreams of the Americas.

Table of Contents

PART TWO
The Stories of Work, Communion, and Selfhood

PART THREE
Work, Communication, and Selfhood

Introduction

The purposes of this book are to make a contribution to the field of communication and to tell the story of the Acadians who left their homes in Canada to live in the United States. The book is intended to contribute to the field of communication in at least three ways: first, provide a descriptive analysis of situated interaction among members of a specific community; second, demonstrate the capacity of communication to transmit the actions, rules, and grammar of a culture that influences what people can and cannot do; and third, highlight the "consequentiality of communication" as described by Cronen (1995). Within that concept, communication is regarded as an inherent feature of living, and not as a simple vehicle for the transmission of messages. Within this framework people are viewed as active participants in creating ways of being, acting, thinking, relating, and feeling. Communication is perceived as an elemental aspect of both the social process and individuality. This study references the consequentiality of communication by looking at situated communication and finding at its center a shared grammar, moral forces, and an active process of coordination among a group of people. The stories of the Acadian Americans, and how working came to have its own grammar and meaning for them, produces testimony of what it is to live a life in the process of communication. This study attempts to understand, examine, and assess these patterns of human communication among Acadian Americans, and describe how their communication led them to become the people that they are. The concept of consequentiality helps to make sense of how they work in certain ways, and that working "hard" is a way of being and acting in their world. Coherence for the Acadian Americans is found in living their everyday lives and the stories they tell about their lived experiences. Coherence is critical to their communication and how the meaning of work has significance in their lives. The book also provides a look into the lives of the Acadian Americans. There are few studies that have focused on this group. In studying their communication practices, stories about their lives emerge.

In working towards these goals the book is presented in three parts. Part one comprises chapters 1 through 4. The intent of this section is to provide the reader with the context for this study. In this section several issues are addressed. First, historical information about the Acadians is presented and more specifically the experiences of Acadians who migrated to the United States. These historical events influenced and continue to influence the meanings behind the stories that are told in the second part of the book. There are a variety of events and actions that are tied to deep beliefs about others, and how a "good person" must act. Secondly, the multiple perspectives of work are presented in chapter 2. As discussed in chapter 3, the vast majority of studies about work are positioned in the received view. There are few studies that have considered work beyond paid employment. The Acadian Americans present a group that does not make distinctions between paid work—employment—and work in other parts of life. In addition, they have constructed a meaning about work that cannot be captured by traditional approaches that look within the individual. This tradition of research has influenced the direction of this book to seek an alternative position to develop an understanding about work. The fourth and final chapter in this section briefly describes American pragmatism and how it grew into an alternative to traditional ways of knowing. American pragmatism was an early effort to offer an alternative to the received view. At the heart of pragmatism is the goal of emancipating humankind from the dominant position of the mind as the central focus of study. American pragmatism offers us meaningful insight into the study of work and its relationship to communication, which is among the central themes of this book. Most importantly, pragmatism has the ability to situate communication as a central feature of what it means to live a life. Pragmatism is valuable in its ability to inform communication research, theory, and practice (Cronen & Chetro-Szivos, 2001). American pragmatism is called on because it serves as a foundation for the Coordinated Management of Meaning (CMM), the communication theory that was called upon to analyze the Acadian-American stories. The last part of the third chapter describes CMM as a practical theory of communication. The philosophical position of pragmatism and the communication theory of CMM provide a lens that addresses the ambiguity and the dynamic nature of work, and a method to analyze the stories the Acadian Americans shared in the interviews. CMM is a methodology capable of entering into this culture and interpreting the stories that the Acadian Americans shared about their lives.

Part two, which comprises Chapters 5 through 9, contains the stories and episodes that make up the lives of the Acadian Americans, and here they speak about their culture and what episodes of interaction are like. The stories and episodes the Acadian Americans share become the central focus of the analysis that follows in Part three. The third section illustrates how the members used communication to construct their understanding of working and other integral aspects of their lives. Above all, we see how working is intrinsic to a way of living for the members of this culture. The interviews with Acadian Americans produced numerous accounts of working that were particular to their lives, family, culture and the enactment of selfhood. These stories show the multiple levels of meaning shared by members of this community, and why working is a central feature of their lives. Each story revealed what the action of "working hard" is like, and the connections of these stories to the Acadian-American culture. By examining how these stories are used in coordinated conversation, it is also possible to understand how these stories are reconstituted and developed.

The analysis of the interviews presented considerable evidence of how people construct social reality and how they construct ideas of truth through interaction and conversation. Furthermore, there is evidence of how these realities and truths are sustained and are subject to change through interaction. The analysis of these stories attempts to understand the experience of these individuals and their strong association with working. The actions of the Acadian Americans and their relationship to work are explored through the stories and episodes they share in the interviews. In this analysis themes and stories of working hard, the right things to do, and the ways a person should and must work clearly emerge in the interactions among the participants in the interviews.

The stories presented here fit into several major themes that the participants raised in the interviews: stories of family, stories of church and school, stories of people who work hard (or what they referred to as motivated people), stories of their lives with non-Acadians, and stories of vacation and leisure time. Within each of these themes there are episodes of living that reveal the rules the members call upon. Sections of the transcripts are provided to show how the members interact and coordinate their action and achieve coherence. The interviews reveal a number of stories about who the Acadian Americans are, would like to be, and what an episode of action is like. These themes, stories, and episodes become the central focus of the analysis that follows.

The transcript in many ways does not capture the energy and sentiment expressed by the participants. The notation and transcription methods cannot express the high level of interaction, laughter, and conviction the members shared during the interviews. The reader may notice the frequent interruptions and emphasis the participants place on certain words and points in the conversation. This is an Acadian-American way of talking which has its own rules that are important in understanding what meanings they bring to interaction. The CMM analysis will describe the forces that influence the action of the members, and it also describes the reflexive effects and reflexive needs that the members call upon. The reflexive effects and reflexive needs are prominent features of this group, and they shape the content of the interviews and the action the members share. Throughout the interviews the reflexive effects are noticeable in the way the members join in the stories with each other. There is a distinctive way of talking, and interruptions are not made in an offensive manner. They are offered as a sign of mutual understanding and commonality. This pattern of communication has its own rules for interaction, which serve to sustain ideas about being an Acadian American and allow the members to create stories in a conjoint process. The members call upon a grammatical ability in telling these stories which develops ideas of what a person is, and what a person should do. Reflexive needs are found in this level of interaction as well. There is a high level of excitement in responding to questions in the interviews and to other participants' comments. As will be shown, the members place a great deal of importance on belonging to this community. What becomes evident is that these Acadian Americans have a need to fit and belong in their community. The coherence within their community can fall apart when viewed from a position outside of the Acadian-American community. Many of their actions differ from practices among members of other cultures, and the larger culture they now live within. Belonging justifies the coherence of their patterns of living and reconstitutes who they are. These concepts will be explored in greater depth below, but are important to keep in mind when reviewing the data.

The third and final part of the book is presented in Chapters Ten and Eleven. In these concluding chapters a discussion is offered to point out how communication is the primary social process because of its capacity to maintain a society, create moments of shared identity through forms of ritual, rules, forces, and meanings. To say that communication is the primary social process is to say that social persons, relations, and institutions are the outcomes of communication. Stories of working are featured prominently in the lives of Acadian Americans.

The analysis of the interviews presented considerable evidence of how people construct social reality, and how they construct ideas of truth through interaction and conversation. Furthermore, there is evidence of how these realities and truths are sustained, and are subject to change through interaction. The analysis of these stories attempts to understand the experience of the Acadian Americans and their strong association to work.

The final chapter offers concluding statements and explores what can be said about work as a result of this study. Here I offer my final thoughts on the contributions Acadian Americans make to understanding working and how people live in and by communication.

Acknowledgments

This book explores the meaning of work by focusing on the grammar of the term *working* among Acadian Americans. I enjoyed the many hours interviewing and interacting with the people you will be introduced to in this book. The analysis of the interviews would not have been as effective without the theory and methodology of the *Coordinated Management of Meaning* (CMM) developed by Vernon Cronen and Barnett Pearce. I am especially indebted to Vernon Cronen, who served as a guide for this work and as a mentor to me. Vernon has given me countless hours of his time, and with kindness and generosity he has inspired me to reach new levels in my thinking and scholarship. Most importantly, I now see the world as made of continuities and not of dichotomies.

I also extend my gratitude to my colleagues at Fitchburg State College, who are always there for me. I am also thankful for the students who indirectly helped me with this project. Their enthusiasm and interest in my work helped me to persevere.

I offer a special thank you to Thea Marcoux for her generous assistance, valuable structural suggestions, and technical expertise. Her contribution at the end of this project was invaluable.

Most of all, I am thankful to the Acadian-American people whose voices speak in the following pages. They willingly shared their ideas, thoughts, and their culture. The Acadian Americans demonstrated how feeling and action organize and symbolize experience. When I read over these pages I have fond memories of them and of their stories and recognize how fortunate I am to live among them. There is something that is inspiring in their ideas of working and living. A phrase they employed often has made my life far richer, and that is: "to make a difference." I can only hope this book can make a contribution to the beautiful story that is theirs, and one day my work too can make a difference.

Gardner, Massachusetts
2006

PART ONE

Background and Foundations

Chapter 1

Working and Its Relation to Communication

THE ORIGINAL INTENT OF THIS BOOK was to present a study of work from a communication perspective. The initial direction came about when I became aware of how few studies have explored the communication practices of workers, or the impact of the recursive nature of communication and its influences on people's experiences of work. There are many studies that focus on the internal dimensions of the worker, and others that focus on people's value orientation toward working as a life role. Within this text communication is not regarded as a simple process of transmission between a sender and receiver, nor is it assumed that there is an objective world of words where all meanings are clear. In this study languages and their meanings are regarded as having an equivocal nature, and an inherent imperfection that allows a multiple world of meanings and possibilities for action. Here communication is considered a form of action that persons perform together, and the reality they live within is made through an ongoing process of interaction.

I chose to study the concept of working among members of the Acadian-American community. The Acadian Americans were selected because of how intently work is featured in their interactions and lives. I recognize that work is not the same in all places, but this is an exceptional starting point to explore the grammar of the term *working* because of its prominence among these people. The Acadian Americans do not represent all cultures, but they show us that the meaning of "working" is not bounded by accomplished tasks. They can show how the meaning of the term extends into rules and practices that are made in interaction among a community of people. I have found the Acadian Americans' understanding of working is much more than of a word with a common definition. In fact it will be shown that working, the act or process as well as the word, has an inseparable link to many aspects of their lives.

Because of the inextricable link between working and the life of an Acadian American, this book also serves as a study of Acadian Americans' culture. For various reasons there is little research devoted to the Acadian-American culture. There are excellent sources that discuss the lives of Franco-Americans, but usually the focus of these works is the experience of the Québécois. The two groups share many similarities, yet they differ in as many significant ways. This text makes a contribution by presenting and analyzing the life stories of Acadian Americans. Their stories provide a meaningful and valuable perspective about their community and how a person lives as a member of this rich and unique culture.

These Acadian-American stories about working show communication as a complex interactive process. The process of communication generates, sustains, or changes meaning among members of a system through recursive interaction. Communication is not simply a vehicle for the exchange of ideas, but an essential feature of living. People act into the world and become who they are because of the constitutive nature of communication. Communication served as the primary social process that allowed these members to construct a grammar, and to live their lives in a coherent and purposeful manner. However, such a view of communication differs from other perspectives that have sought to find descriptive and predictive aspects of communication. Instead, this study focused on the reflexive and recursive features of communication among the Acadian Americans. Part two will provide evidence of the reflexive features of communication as members extended Acadian American stories, and lived as active participants in a community they shared with others. Belonging to this community means they live their lives in accordance with rules and practices that are coherent to the members of the community. The recursive features of communication indicated the episodes that compose social reality were created by the actors, and then this social reality served as the context for the actions of the actors (Pearce & Cronen, 1980). It is within these episodes, which are made up of shared rules and conjoint actions, that the actors live and create their social reality. This social reality they have created is replete with morals and forces that direct their action. The Acadian American episodes of interaction show that human action is conjoint action, which is to say that what we do is influenced by the interests and desires, and by the actions of those around us.

The assumption of this study is that communication is not set apart from people's beliefs and actions. The stories here are not regarded as simple accounts of their lives. Instead, these stories reveal how the Acadian Americans construct and sustain both community and selfhood, which comprise their beliefs of what it is to be a good Acadian American. These situated interactions substantiate the grammar, logical forces, and meanings of living an Acadian-American story of working. This study examined these rules, forces, meanings, and the process that Acadian Americans used to construct the world they live in to and develop this unique meaning of working.

Again summarizing this book's structure: Part one provides the grounding for this work. In this section a description of the Acadian experience is provided, which includes relevant historical information. There is an overview explaining how major fields of study have conceptualized work. Part one concludes with an introduction to American pragmatism and its influence on the Coordinated Management of Meaning, the communication theory that informed the analysis of the Acadian American stories. Part two contains the stories and episodes that make up the lives of the Acadian Americans; here they speak about their culture and what episodes of interaction are like. The stories and episodes the Acadian Americans share becomes the central focus of the analysis that follows in part three. The third section illustrates how the members used communication to construct their understanding of working, and other integral aspects of their lives. Above all, we see how working is intrinsic to a way of living for the members of this culture.

The Meaning of Work

Work is a common institution found in all cultures, yet there seems to be a taken-for-granted position when it comes to understanding what working means. A richer understanding of what working means to different people and in different places is needed. This is made even more compelling as the work force becomes more diverse in its composition. However, the meaning of the term *work* is ambiguous. The literature on the meaning of work is extensive, but it is fragmented as the research has diverged in several directions. The concept in most cases describes a general set of beliefs about work held by an individual. It is widely held that a person's orientation toward work is acquired through a process of socialization. However work is most often measured by exploring career interests, job performance, longevity, absenteeism, alienation, and job satisfaction, which are all internal personal dimensions. These are all measures of behavior relevant to a specific job that occurs in a specific context. Yet there is agreement among most researchers that a well-articulated theory of the meaning of working, based on conceptually sound understanding of the meaning of working itself with the ability of yielding clear cut policy implications is not available (MOW International Research Team., 1987). *The American Heritage Dictionary* provides forty-three noun and verb definitions, and the *Oxford English Dictionary* dedicates over a page to define the term *work*. Clearly, it is difficult to articulate what work means. The complexity of the definition may indicate that working does not have the same meaning and function for all people, or that research methods to date have not been able to express this concept fully. I hope to explore both of these concepts by engaging the members of a community where work has such a prominent place in members' lives.

Work in many ways serves as the basis of social order as it is well institutionalized as a prominent feature of life in industrial and service-based economies. It is apparent that work is inextricably woven into the fabric of what it is to live a life. I was surprised, in light of how prevalent work is in society, to find that the scope of the literature about working lacks a clear definition. There is substantial research that attempts to capture the meaning of work by studying individuals' work values. There are studies that examine the importance of work in people's lives by making use of the concepts of work involvement and work salience. There is another focus that measures the effect of work alienation. Yet these directions have not yielded a clear conception of what work is. Most importantly, there is a limited pool of research that explores the notion of a grammar of working, or approaches work in a systematic manner.

The study of work has been further complicated as existing attempts to study it have divided work into paid employment and non-paid work, which generally refers to work done in the home. The majority of researchers have focused on paid employment when studying work and working. This separation has yielded research that looks at only one dimension of working and neglects to look at the concept of work in its totality. The scope of this book is to study the effect and the action of working, not its intent. This study will approach work as a system, and not as a thing that occurs simply as paid employment. In so doing, this study is grounded in a communication systems approach, and particularly the philosophy of American pragmatism. The Coordinated Management of Meaning (CMM), an outgrowth of pragmatism, was selected as a communication theory and methodology used to collect and analyze data. Through this study I hope to expand ideas about the concept of working, and suggest some possible ways to think of work and its larger implications.

This research uses the theory of CMM (Pearce & Cronen, 1980; Cronen, 1994) to provide a critical interpretation of interviews with Acadian Americans. The CMM analysis will illustrate the ways in which the communicative practices of this group create, reaffirm, and change the meaning of work for its members. This analysis will attempt to describe the importance and influence of the stories lived and told by Acadian Americans, their understandings, constructions, actions, and obligations to work in a particular way. Within this study, the CMM analysis and discussion of the interviews will be supported by research that focuses on the rules people call upon in situated action as described by Wittgenstein (1958); the moral forces that influence what people can and cannot do as discussed by Cronen (1994), and communication as the primary social process as discussed by Dewey (1916).

The Grammar of Working

This is not an ethnographic study of Acadian Americans. This study will explore the grammar of work among the Acadian-American population, and address the formative aspects of grammar within that human system. In studying the grammar of work, the concern is with the role of working and the connection working has to the life of these people. The concept of a grammar of working is based on Wittgenstein's notion that grammar includes the rules people use to create an episode that is coherent to members of a group. Grammar refers not only to words, sentences, and paragraphs, but also to gestures, emotions and patterns of behavior (Wittgenstein, 1958). A grammar of working has to do with the way talk about working and working itself are organized so that Acadian Americans know how to "go on" in conversation. A grammar is learned by acting with others in a way that is coherent and makes sense to the participants of that system.

The rules of working for Acadian Americans differ from many other cultures. To begin with, when Acadian Americans talk about working their talk is not limited to paid employment. Acadian Americans work in the same ways at home, in the community, and at their jobs. Their grammar of working also includes themes of honesty and pride. The study will illustrate that Acadian Americans have ideas of the right ways of working, which are what a "motivated person" does, and share a common understanding of the ways a person should not work. Within the Acadian American's grammar there are conceptions of acting as a motivated person, doing it for yourself, making a difference, and making the best of all situations. These are important features of the Acadian American grammar of working.

Cultures are extremely complex and the intent here is to focus on one distinctive aspect among members of a community who show a deep pride and commitment to the notion of working. This book will introduce ideas to study the grammar of working which may be applied to other cultural groups to help understand the concept of working, a prominent aspect in the lives of most people. Work is vitally important in what it is to live a life, and it is not the same in all places. I am not going to answer the importance of work for all cultures; instead I will offer a detailed analysis of a unique situation and demonstrate the meanings the term takes on for members of a particular culture.

The Coordinated Management of Meaning

CMM, influenced by the work of the American pragmatists, regards communication as the primary social process. CMM presents a communication theory and a methodology to enter into the activity of people with the intent of understanding and enriching experience by making sense of the fluid character of everyday conversation. This CMM analysis of interviews with Acadian Americans will reveal the propositions of the theory detailed in chapter 3. The analysis will explore the stories lived and told by members about working which will reveal individual and group identity. As we explore the stories, the meaning of the term *working* and what it means to work hard will be illustrated. Critical to this analysis are the perceived, spoken, and unspoken communication, and the forces that influence both talk and action. Lastly, the influence of the researcher and research methodology on the outcome of the interviews will be explored.

The communication practices of the Acadian Americans are the focus of the study. Entering into their practices and grammar was accomplished through the use of circular questioning. In the interview process, each response to a question was followed by another question which intended not only to provide information, but allowed the participants to see connections between beliefs and actions. There are moments in the interviews where the participants began to gain awareness, ask questions of each other, and raise apparent contradictions in their stories. This study explored those moments that illustrate communication as the primary social process by which transmission of meaning is possible.

Conversation serves as the basic unit of observation, but it is the episodes of interaction that are the basic unit of social analysis (Cronen, 1995a). CMM focuses on interaction because all social action is organized within episodes, and in these episodes rules and practices that are a part of the participants' grammatical abilities reside. A CMM analysis is focused on discovering the structure, patterns, rules, and stories participants use. A concern of CMM is how stories attain coherence among people. This may be understood by exploring the interaction between levels of context, episode, selfhood, and culture. While the analysis focuses on situated interaction, Pearce (1989) reminds us that interaction occurs within a larger network of action. The interactions that are the focus of this analysis may only be understood in terms of the larger network they are a part of. The interactions must be analyzed in terms of the Acadian-American stories of family, culture, work, and church. The significance of these aspects of their lives will be described fully in the third part of the book

Reflexivity

CMM provides a way to observe the reflexivity that Acadian Americans share in the stories of working. Throughout the interviews the reflexive effects are noticeable in the way that members would join with each other in the stories. Their distinctive patterns of talking had their own rules for interaction, which served to sustain ideas about living an Acadian American story. The communication also provided the members with opportunities to create stories within a conjoint process of action. The members called upon their grammatical abilities in telling stories that developed notions of what a person is, and what a person should do. There was evidence of reflexive needs found within the interaction among the members as well, and a high level of excitement in responding to interview questions and to other participants. The members placed a great deal of importance on belonging to this community. What became evident was that there is a need to fit and belong. The Acadian Americans work, celebrate their families, and have a relationship with their community that is unique. When viewed from the outside, their actions may not make sense to others. It became evident that belonging is important to the members. It is belonging that justi-fies the coherence of their patterns of living, and this belonging helps to recon-stitute who they are.

The Aesthetics of Experience, Logical Forces and Moral Orders

This study attempts to account for the aesthetics of experience. The Acadian Americans told stories about when working feels good, and how working is what a person lives for. What the members felt should not be overlooked. The aesthetics reveal how working is so prominent for Acadian Americans. The interviews showed how feeling and action organize and symbolize experi-ence. There is a consummatory experience that comes about for them through working, and the other members understood these moving experi-ences. The consummatory experiences provided a heightened sense of iden-tity and membership in a community of people that act and feel a certain way about working.

The study shows that the choices people make about what should and should not be done are evidence of the competence required of living in social worlds. This social competence is made up of the rules and practices into which we are socialized. CMM as a methodology regards these rules as constituting a moral order that is the basis of coherence among people living together in action. Communication is guided by the forces for action and moral orders. As a person acts into the world they must achieve coherence and are aware that consequences will result from what is said. The logical forces and moral orders in a given context guide episodes of interaction.

The Acadian Americans' actions are guided by strong logical and moral forces that tell them what a person must be doing, and for what reasons. These forces come from the intertwined relationships among family, culture, work, and church. It was common for the Acadian Americans in this study to talk about the strong obligations to work hard at all things in their lives. While forces such as these may not be unique to this group of people, the study will show episodes where these logical forces and moral orders are enacted, and how they serve to direct and reaffirm specifically Acadian-American stories of living. The bond among the members in the study extended far beyond a shared history. They shared a story of what it is to live a life as an Acadian American with its consistent rules and forces for action. The stories of the past were about fathers who made the best of life while working long hours in the mills, or mothers working for their families for long hours without rest. There are present day stories of men and women losing jobs due to corporate downsizing, but they move onto others jobs that others may consider lesser jobs, and they continue to work hard. Working hard is what a good person does; the forces and moral orders these people share, and have made together in communication, tell them this is the right way to live.

Talking with Acadian Americans

The data for this book was compiled through the use of the circular interviews with different groups of Acadian Americans. The connection among all of the people who were interviewed was membership in the church Notre Dame du Saint Rosaire (Our Lady of the Holy Rosary) in Gardner, Massachusetts. The participants all attended the parochial school that is a part of the church and grew up in the neighborhood surrounding the church, or another section of this city referred to as "Little Canada" (Malloy, 1984).

The analysis comes from the transcript of interviews. The interviews addressed similar areas and topics, but were each unique as the circular questioning followed the course of the interaction among the participants. When possible, noteworthy pauses, intonations, expressions, and nonverbal aspects of the interaction when it affected the content or the flow of the conversation are indicated. The interviews were conducted in English, but some responses were given partly in French. In the second part of the book the reader will be presented with several selections from the interviews with the Acadian Americans. This data is representative of the patterns of talk and the most significant junctures in the conversations. These interactions are indicative of moral orders, rules, practices, and conventions that make up the grammars of Acadian Americans. It is through this interaction that we see how meanings are created in communication, and the numerous forces and levels of meaning that influence the actions of Acadian Americans. There were instances within the interactions that reveal the tensions in enacting Acadian-American stories of working and other relevant topics of family life, culture, or community. These interactions were presented to demonstrate the way that tensions and conflicts, or points of coherence are used to either reaffirm Acadian American stories of working, or change the stories lived or told. Through the analysis of these stories it becomes clear how a concept such as working is produced through the interaction of the members of a community and how Acadian–American selfhood is coordinated within their culture.

The stories shared by the Acadian Americans show how the grammar of working was created and is sustained through a cultural system. If we listen intently, the voices of the Acadian Americans describe how working is what a good person does and how central working is in living a life with others.

Chapter 2

The Acadian Americans

Each fall congregants of Notre Dame du Saint Rosaire (Our Lady of the Holy Rosary), a Catholic church located in Gardner, Massachusetts, stage a fair to raise funds for the support of the church and its elementary school. This annual event has been an important part of the community, one that members of the church have shared for nearly half a century. The church has served Acadians and Acadian Americans, along with others who emigrated from Canada, for the past one hundred years. The Acadians are people who came from Eastern Canada, generally to find work. The majority of the Acadians came in the twentieth century to the city of Gardner to work in its mills. At the church fair, the items that draw the most interest, and generate the most funds, are prepared dishes of traditional Acadian foods. I initially entered this community as a participant-observer and volunteered by helping with food preparation. On my first day at the fair, I stood in line peeling potatoes with approximately twenty members of the church. The talk around the table was about work. Members recounted and shared their stories about their first jobs, best jobs, and difficulties they had encountered while working. There was laughter and joking about how hard they, and other members of their community work. The Acadian Americans even talked about how "outrageous" their actions must appear to others outside of their community.

I have lived among Acadian Americans for several years, and when I have been with Acadian Americans, I am deeply struck with their talk about working, how much of their life story is about working, and how important working appears to be to them as members of a community. There is something interesting about how pervasive the term work is among members of this community, and their awareness that their ways of working are different from those of others. As will be shown, "working" refers to more than a paid job for the Acadian Americans. Working, and especially working hard, is a way of being in this culture. Personal success and competence are not measured by what a group member does for work, but by how hard they work at it. Work extends beyond the boundaries of a job and touches leisure time, social life, and family life.

The People of Acadia

The term *Acadian* refers to the people who settled in the areas known as the Canadian Maritimes, which includes Nova Scotia, New Brunswick, Prince Edward Island, the Madeline Islands of Quebec, and the eastern portion of Maine.[1] The population was made up mostly of migrants from France and some from England who lived along with the Micmac Native Americans and a few other smaller native tribes. It is important to understand that Acadia was not New France, nor was it an extension of New England. Acadia was a distinct third settlement, located between New France and New England. Acadia had great strategic and economic value. The North Atlantic coast offered active ports for ships to explore new lands, fishing was exceptional, and it was the entry to inland waterways beginning with the Saint Lawrence River. Acadia was a much smaller settlement than New France, or the settlements in what is now the United States. Changes in European ideas, and the changes in England and France's power over the new colonies perhaps affected Acadia more than other areas of the North America. The most far-reaching effect on Acadia was its changing status as a colony of either France or England. Sovereignty over Acadia changed several times between the two nations, and did not reach resolution until early in the eighteenth century.

A strong sense of independence developed among the inhabitants while Acadia was considered a colony of France. This is in part due to the lack of support France extended to the settlers. This lack of involvement allowed the settlers to adopt their own customs and means of internal governance. The Treaty of Utrecht in 1713 resolved the issue of who had control over Acadia, England gaining control of it along with other territories held by France. However, by the close of the seventeenth century a recognizable and separate identity had emerged among the Acadians. This identity was a blend of social, cultural, and political variables that were unique to this group of people and distinct from life in New France, New England, or Europe. There were specific ways of organizing community life, providing food and shelter and forming the ideas of the next generation (Griffiths, 1992).

The Treaty of Utrecht required that the Acadians swear an oath to the King of England, but it allowed them to remain neutral toward France and the Micmac tribe. This neutrality agreement lasted for several decades. However, there was a growing discomfort in the British government about the distinct Acadian identity. This concern led to the confiscation of Acadian lands and property, and the systematic deportation of Acadians. The Acadians were forcibly dispersed among the British colonies from Massachusetts to Georgia. A small group of Acadians was sent to Louisiana and another to France. The intent was to dispel the Acadian identity, which was seen as somehow a threat to the Crown. Many Acadians avoided deportation by fleeing to the woods and finding refuge and help from the Micmac. The Micmac supported the Acadians by helping them escape to Quebec or to settlements in New France.

The exile to the colonies proved traumatic for the Acadian population. They suffered horrifying losses; the transport ships used to carry the Acadians were overcrowded and did not have enough rations. This process resulted in the loss of many lives. When the surviving Acadians arrived at their appointed destinations, many contracted smallpox or yellow fever. The dispersal was responsible for the death of more than twenty-five percent of the Acadian population, which had totaled approximately 13,000.

The Acadians petitioned the governments of France and England for relief due to the loss of loved ones and property. As a result, they were allowed to return to the Maritimes. In 1766 more than two hundred families walked back to the Maritimes from Massachusetts (Rose, 1953). The fertile lands they once held in Nova Scotia had been claimed by new settlers in their absence, and the English government imposed restrictions on the Acadians to keep the settlements powerless. Eventually the majority of Acadians resettled in New Brunswick and isolated themselves from the English and from the government of Canada (Daigle, 1982; Griffiths, 1973). The Acadian community exists today mostly in the province of New Brunswick. As recently as 1972 an Acadian political party was formed in Canada.

Migration from New Brunswick

The Acadians continued their isolation until an outward migration began in the 1880s and continued through the 1960s. The move from New Brunswick was caused by persistent economic depression and dislocation. The Acadian people in the Province of New Brunswick suffered economically while central and western Canada prospered. Migration drew Acadians to the urban areas of western Canada, and a large number of Acadians moved to the United States to work in the mills of New England (Brookes, 1976). Seventy-two percent of the French Canadians who emigrated to the United States in 1912 lived in New England (Harney, 1982). The emigration of French-speaking Canadians included both the Québécois from the province of Quebec, and the Acadians from New Brunswick. The Acadians' customs and practices differed significantly from the Québécois, as they originated from rural areas and were far poorer than the Québécois. Many of the stories gathered in this study talk about the level of poverty among Acadian immigrants as late as the 1960s. Harney characterized the acceptance of the French Canadians in New England as without hostility. The French Canadians did not compete for jobs in municipal government that other ethnic groups coveted; instead, like the Québécois before them, the Acadians worked the long hours and less desirable jobs in the mills, and had limited involvement with local politics and issues. This theme of working hard and disconnecting from people competing for power remains constant in the story of Acadian life. The Acadian immigrants were treated very differently from the immigrants who came from Europe, who received more attention in efforts to Americanize them. Harney stated "the danger in being French-Canadian was less one of being assaulted and insulted and more one of being ignored in poverty and exploitation" (pg. 84). Statistics on immigration showed that the French-Canadians led all other groups in ability to use the English language, but the data showed that they continued to speak French at home and in their immediate community and neighborhood (Fishman, 1981).

Life in the New England Towns

The Acadians lived in close-knit neighborhoods often referred to as "Little Canada." These neighborhoods were commonly found in the New England mill towns of the late nineteenth and twentieth centuries. These neighborhoods offered affordable housing and a strong sense of community with the Catholic church as the prominent feature of community and family life, especially when the church offered a French-speaking priest. Harney points out that there are few social science studies of the Little Canadas, which he felt could be attributed to the scarcity of Franco Americans who went on to graduate studies in history and the social sciences.

The French Canadian population of Salem, Massachusetts, in Harvey's study parallels the Acadian community found in this study in the city of Gardner, Massachusetts. In this study, the French Catholic church is the dominant feature of this community. Notre Dame du Saint Rosaire (Our Lady of the Holy Rosary) was established in 1884 and opened a parochial school almost immediately. The school closed for short time in 1896 but was reopened in 1903 with 500 students (Clark, 1988). Gardner had two neighborhoods where the majority of the Acadians settled along with the Québécois from Canada. The immediate area around the church housed approximately 500 families, and Little Canada, which was within a mile of the church, housed approximately another 500 families (Malloy, 1984; Moore, 1967; Rose, 1953).

The neighborhoods are made up of largely tenement blocks and a few small private homes. These tenements provided affordable housing for emigrants from the late 1800s through the 1960s. The buildings are crowded together without yards; they were built primarily to house mill workers. The design and construction of the buildings were based on function more than aesthetics, and they offered few amenities. While these houses and apartment blocks resemble

buildings found in poorer urban areas, the families that remain in the neighborhood to this day maintain the houses to a high standard of cleanliness and
order.

These French-speaking neighborhoods of Gardner were a mix of the
Québécois and the Acadians. The Québécois migrated to Gardner in the late
nineteenth century, before the Acadians. Most of the Acadians came to Gardner
in the twentieth century. Rose indicated there were only 225 Acadians in Gardner in 1905, more than 400 Acadian families in Gardner by 1922, and 2,121
Acadians in the city by 1930. By 1960 the Acadians were estimated at more
than 4,000 people in a city of approximately 20,000.[2] Rose and several other
historians have noted, the extent of the Acadian immigration is difficult to
determine because the census did not distinguish Acadians, but grouped them
with the people from Quebec as French Canadian; later in the twentieth century both are referred to as the ethnic category "Franco-American." There is
little descriptive data available about Acadian Americans due to this classification (Choquette, L., personal communication, March 15, 2000). Estimates are
that within Gardner the majority of the Franco-American population is of
Acadian origin. Rose, writing in the 1950s, estimated the Acadian population
in New England at about 100,000, but emigration from New Brunswick continued into the mid 1960s with more than 60,000 people leaving New
Brunswick between 1961 and 1971 (Daigle, 1982). While the Acadians and
Québécois shared a language and religious beliefs, Rose reported that they had
distinct accents and customs. Due to the isolation in New Brunswick, the Acadians lagged behind the Québécois in education and cultural development. It is
apparent that within this new category of people called Franco-Americans
many significant differences existed. However, the two groups appeared to live
together in relative harmony.[3]

Moore (1967) described the Franco-Americans in Gardner as loyal to the
church, proud of their French heritage, and conversant in the French language.
In addition, Moore characterized them as maintaining strong ties with their
homeland. Moore does not make a distinction between the Acadians and
Québécois, but, as Rose stated, the Acadians were the majority among Franco-
Americans in the city of Gardner.

The church and school preserved their culture, and in time the Franco-
Americans took an active role in politics and businesses of this city. The Acadians shared many clubs and fraternal organizations with the Québécois, but they
also formed their own organizations, such as the Acadian Social Club, which
remains an active part of the community. Within these neighborhoods several
small businesses were owned and operated by Franco-Americans. To this day
there is a thriving credit union that initially focused on serving the French-
speaking population, which has since extended its services to the larger community. The church still has an active membership and sponsors several

women's, men's, and youth associations for members of the congregation. The church remains the principal institution and continues to have a significant influence on the Acadian community. In many ways this church plays an active role in the transmission and maintenance of many of the cultural practices of the Acadian community, which will be demonstrated in the interviews. During the interviews the members talked about having an awareness that being Acadian was to be different from others, including the Québécois. Members stated that as children they had accepted the fact that people called them French Canadian or Franco-American, but in time there grew much more of an interest in knowing about their distinct culture and Acadian identity.[4]

There are still many mill towns, or former mill towns, throughout New England where the Acadian population thrives. Most of the mills have closed, but many Acadians settled in New England while continuing to maintain close ties to families in New Brunswick. I refer to the people in this book as Acadian-American because they have lived in the United States for the majority of their lives. These people attended school, work at jobs, and raise families in the United States. The Catholic church as a center of Acadian community life is not unique to these people. This is a common occurrence in the locations where the Acadians have settled. All of the participants in the study were members of Notre Dame du Saint Rosaire, located in Gardner, Massachusetts, and as children attended its school. All of the people interviewed lived within the Acadian neighborhoods during their childhood.

The intention of this book is to contribute to an understanding about working by studying the grammar of the term. As indicated in the introduction, the Acadian Americans were selected because of how intently work is featured in their interactions and lives. This is not an ethnographic study of Acadian American culture. Instead, this study explores how social practices are created in and by communication, and forms of life and selfhood emerge from interaction. The grammar of working and the grammatical abilities of Acadian Americans can be approached and analyzed to reveal the rules and practices they call upon in situated interaction to develop an understanding of working. What is particularly interesting about the Acadian Americans is the inextricable link that exists between work and other aspects of their culture. The relationship of working to their construction of a community and self is deeply embedded in their story of life in North America.

Chapter 3

Perspectives of Work

Historical Perspectives of Work

Throughout history work has had a variety of meanings and levels of importance to society and individuals. Tilgher (1962) traced the historical directions of work and showed the many positions work has taken. The ancient Greeks regarded work as a curse, or at best a necessary evil, reserved for slaves and the poor. The influences of religious indoctrination changed perspectives toward work. The Judeo-Christian traditions have shaped the view of work that is most commonly found in western nations. The Hebrews held the belief that work was painful, but it was a necessity and punishment for original sin. Early Christians conceptualized work as a means for redemption, and that it served to fulfill noble ends. The splintering of Christian beliefs into various sects stimulated different views about living, and conceptions of work figured prominently in these religious movements. Catholicism stressed the positive aspects of work and regarded work as good for the moral and spiritual integrity of people. Work was antithetical to leisure and idleness, which brought about weakness and corruption. The Reformation produced glorification of work, as seen in the doctrines of Lutheranism and Calvinism. Luther preached working hard and devoutly as the best way to serve God. A job was thought of as a calling and the path to salvation. Calvin regarded work as a religious obligation; working hard was seen as the highest virtue humans can attain. The Calvinist tradition held that people must work hard, but also warned of the danger of enjoying the products of their efforts in this world. The teachings of Luther and Calvin provided a moral code that became known as the Protestant Ethic. Under this perspective pleasure and idleness are regarded with disdain. The goal of work became the perfection of an occupation. The ethic served as a guide of conduct that pervades all aspects of life. God was thought of as demanding a life of good *works*, and these works were incorporated into a system with *labor* and *vocation* as central features. Labor was elevated from a series of mundane tasks to a calling. This idea of a calling differed from the traditional Catholic morality of monastic piety. A calling provided an opportunity for all people to have a highly individualized relationship with God through labor. A highly individualized relationship augmented the western ideas of individualism and of the mind as the center of experience. We see in the writings of Weber (1958) a strong relationship between the Protestant Ethic and the basis of order in capitalist economies. Weber felt the spirit of the Protestant Ethic and capitalism mesh in the vocational culture that grew out of this moral code (Habermas, 1984). Work holds a position of prominence in contemporary western societies as it permeates the life of people in society.

The Roman Catholic position with regard to work is relevant to this study, as the Acadian Americans are predominantly Roman Catholic, and in the data collection it was discovered that Catholicism plays a major role in their lives and in their grammar of working.[1] Features of Roman Catholic sacraments such as Communion and Penance were described in episodes of interaction between the Acadian Americans.[2]

The writings of several Roman Catholic popes have been dedicated to the theme of work in the encyclicals of Leo XII, *Rerum Novarum,* 1891, Pius XI, *Qudragesimo Anno,* 1931, and more recently an encyclical of John Paul II, *Laboreum exercens,* 1981. John Paul II's encyclical came on the ninetieth anniversary of Leo XII's encyclical. Both documents addressed the Church's position on work. In the 1981 Papal letter, John Paul II postulates that humans are placed on earth to work and subdue the earth. He professed that work is an activity that distinguishes humans from other living creatures. The activities of other creatures are necessary for their existence, but it is not work in the sense of subduing nature and advancing relations between a species and its environment (John Paul II, 1981). Although work consists of toil and suffering, the Church's contention is that it is through work that people derive dignity. People cultivate resources and go beyond themselves in the process of working. Work is conceived of as a fundamental dimension of man's existence on earth. John Paul II pointed to the Book of Genesis as the source of a conviction that links work with human existence. Within the Book of Genesis man is directed by the Creator to fill the earth and subdue it, and humans subdue the earth through labor. Humans are regarded as subjects of work, performing actions that belong to the work process and these actions serve to advance humanity. Work is seen as a means for people to join God in the process of creation by transforming the world. John Paul II viewed the creation itself as a form of work done by God during six days. He noted that the New Testament describes Christ as toiling at the carpenter's bench, and again toiling in the work of salvation that led to his death. Christ's sacrifice is seen as a collaboration between humans and the Son of God for the redemption of humanity.

Toil is universally known to the farmer, laborer, scientist, and to parents. The Catholic Church regards this as a universal calling. This calling is seen as necessary because it assists in transforming nature and serves as a means to forward human existence. John Paul II stressed the moral obligation of work and the connection between the virtue of industriousness and the importance of social order. He found that work makes family life possible through the means of subsistence, and work promotes the advance of society and individual dignity. The Catholic viewpoint sees work as a duty demanded by the Creator which maintains and develops humanity.

Work has become a necessity as well as a duty, and is highly regarded in contemporary societies. The Judeo-Christian influences on work include views of work as punishment for original sin, work as a duty to God and community, work leading to character development, leading to a closer relationship to God, and work as an act of creation.

The Study of Work

The classical literature on work largely focuses on studying the psyche of the individual worker and the importance of the psychological function of work. The aims of most studies are to locate the intrinsic meaning of the work experience, and measure its influence as a source of identity and self-esteem. This is not an unusual starting point for Western researchers who have been deeply influenced by Cartesian ideas of inner and outer dichotomies, and the logical positivist approaches that make the individual the fundamental unit of analysis. This approach, which is consistent with the received view, seeks to decipher the social world by dividing it into smaller units of individuals, and again by reducing the individuals into factors like intentions, attitudes, perceptions, and cognition. This view encompasses the belief that there is a set of stable relationships capable of revealing universal laws that tell us about the subject matter. There are concerns about the capacity of this view when it applies to social issues that are as complex and ambiguous as work. The remainder of this chapter provides a comparative review of the traditional positions and alternative positions that have been offered as related to the meaning of work. The first part of the review will present a selective review of traditional approaches, which include psychological and sociological theories of work. This will include an explanation of its research orientations and theoretical assumptions. A brief review is provided of efforts by communication researchers to make sense of work.

Traditional Views

Research by social scientists regarding work has taken three general directions. Some efforts try to derive the meaning of work by studying individuals' work values. or goals they attempt to attain through their work. Another means is to examine the importance of work in peoples' lives by measuring levels of work involvement or work salience. The third approach is to analyze the degree to which people feel estranged from workplaces. This later concept is referred to as work alienation (Sverko & Vidovek, 1995). It is clear that many efforts to research work have focused on internal dynamics of the individual who goes to a specific place to perform a job. What we know about work has been gathered by careful observations and the measurement of concrete social facts. As will be shown in the following pages, the researchers will seek to discover an overarching framework that will explain and enhance understandings of human life. The traditional view is steeped in a concentration on empirical facts, and it is believed that the objectivism will garner explanations that apply to a wide range of circumstances. The goal of such research is the ability to articulate universal laws that describe what behaviors people enact in the world.

Work Values

The research that is focused on studying individuals' work values generally describes values as an organized set of beliefs, opinions, and attitudes about what people prefer as right. Most of these researchers recognize values as hypothetical constructs that cannot be directly observed. The assessment of values is achieved through examination of individual preferences for different aspects of work content and context. The research questions are often focused on what people seek in their jobs, which values dominate their work lives, and whether workers are motivated by self-fulfillment or economic rewards. Most commonly, studies of work values relied on measures of economic security, material rewards, social status and self-fulfillment through job titles and duties. Sverko points out that most studies try to assess the importance of factors such as job context or the meaning of work itself in relation to external values such as physical conditions or wages.

There is a literature on studies done early on in the field of applied psychology. Psychologists were seeking ways to understand work values and their relationship to motivation. These researchers focused their studies on people's interests as an indicator of values. They developed psychological instruments that have been used extensively for several decades (Fryer, 1931; Strong, 1943) in areas such as interest and preference testing. More recently research has continued in the areas of needs, values, and interests. These concepts are grouped together and are thought of as a valid psychological construct (Super, 1995). The general consensus among most researchers is that these studies have not produced definitive answers, or identified common priorities for people who work.

Work Involvement

Work involvement studies are thought to provide a quantitative perspective of the meaning of work. Factors such as the amount of time spent in work activities are commonly used as measures of how involved a person is with work. There are several orientations among the principal researchers who studied work involvement. The principal directions have been that of the authors who described work involvement as intrinsically motivated (Lodahl, 1965), and that of authors who regarded work involvement as the degree to which job satisfaction is central to the person or constitutes a psychological identification with work (Dubin, 1956; Lawler & Hall, 1970; Saleh, 1981). These two orientations were noted by Rabinowitz and Hall (1977) who saw one orientation as describing work involvement as an aspect of self-image and a value orientation toward working as a life role, and the other orientation describing work involvement as a decision orientation, about preferred behaviors. The distinction is made between identification with work, and involvement with or commitment to work. Work identification is seen as the effect of a cognitive consistency process that occurs when comparisons are made between work as an activity and perceptions of self. The general belief is that identification with working emerges as a result of this process. On the other hand, commitment to work is regarded as an affective response to working as a part of a person's life. It is generally believed that these responses can be distinguished in behaviors such as hours at work.

Work involvement was studied extensively in the Meaning of Work Study[3] (MOW International Research Team, 1987) and was described there as "work centrality." Work centrality was defined as a "general belief about the value of working in one's life" (p. 17). The team did not see a distinction between the two research orientations, and they viewed work identification and work involvement/commitment as mutually reinforcing. This team developed two measures of work centrality. The first measure rated the importance of work, and the second measure compared work importance with other life areas such as family, religion, community and leisure. This approach corresponds to other studies that examined central life interests (Dubin, 1956), theory of behavioral settings (Barker, 1968), theory of interpersonal relationships (Heider, 1958), and work in relation to other life roles (Super, 1980). The team concluded that value orientations and decision orientations of work centrality should be combined to provide a more complete conceptualization of work centrality to determine the general belief of the value of working in a person's life. They felt that work centrality is a measure based on cognition and affects which are indicative of the degree of importance that working has to a particular person.

Defining the construct of work involvement has come under criticism largely due to the ambiguity of the concept of work involvement itself. Most prominent of the critics of the work involvement literature is Kanungo, who points to the indistinct definition of work involvement on three points: First, it does not distinguish between involvement with a particular job and involvement with work in general. Second, problems arise in an inadequate distinction between work involvement and intrinsic motivation. Finally, it was not clear whether job involvement was a cognitive or an affective state; Kanungo assumed that work involvement is primarily a cognitive state of the person's identification with work, and affect and behaviors are consequences of the cognitive state (Kanungo, 1979, 1982). Sverko and Vidiveck (1995) pointed out that Kanungo's critique was the catalyst for research that proceeded in three main directions. The first group of researchers felt work involvement was determined by individual variables; they examined relationships among various characteristics such as age, sex, income level, education, marital status and other personality traits. The second category of research regarded work involvement as a situational variable and studied the intrinsic motivation influenced by characteristics such as management style, position and formality of the hierarchy, and the relationships between supervisors and subordinates. The third group of researchers focused on consequences of work involvement by measuring job satisfaction, and performance. Rabinowitz and Hall (1977) provided a listing of the attributes of the job-involved person. Among the attributes that they articulated are: (a) belief in the Protestant ethic; (b) an internal locus of control; (c) strong growth needs; (d) has a job which provides a high degree of autonomy, variety, and feedback; (e) actively participates in decision making that affect her/him; history of success; (f) is satisfied with the job; and (g) is unlikely to leave the organization. These attributes are consistent with traditional approaches that attempt to understand work by exploring the inner mind of the individual and identifying the essential elements of behavior.

Work Alienation

Work has been studied from a third perspective, and that is the concept of alienation—when work becomes meaningless to individuals. This concept is largely tied to Marxist and Neo-Marxist theories that claim that conditions of a capitalistic economy and industrialization inhibit the realization of being human and lead to alienation from work and life itself. Wilensky (1981) described work alienation as a feeling that the routine enactment of the obligations and rights of a person's work role are inconsistent with the person's self-image. A measure of work alienation is completed by measuring the central attributes of the self-concept to which the person attaches strong positive affects. Among early empirical investigations of alienation were those done by Seeman (1959) who constructed alienation as a multidimensional variable consisting of the five components powerlessness, meaninglessness, anomie, isolation, and self-estrangement. Most researchers studying work alienation have adopted these dimensions. There is little agreement among authors about the concept of alienation itself. Rus and Arzensek (1984) claimed the concept of alienation not only has various meanings to different authors but it is used to explain different concepts, social problems, and life-style tendencies.

Critique of Traditional Approaches

The perspectives discussed above share a foundational belief that individual attributes and veiled psychological processes are the factors to be discovered. It is felt that these discussions will serve as the basis of explanation for laws of human behavior and work itself. Within this framework, people are thought of as stable and predictable with a strong sense of independence and autonomy. Personality and its traits are the central focus of a "mechanical self," a term coined by Gergen (1973). A mechanical self emerges as people are seen as products of rewards, situational demands, or social pressures merged with institutional influences to produce personal dispositions. In this logical positivist frame, character, disposition, and personality traits are thought of as enduring and capable of guiding peoples' actions throughout their lives. The "mechanical self" is predictable because behavior is regarded as reliable and stable across most situations. Personality, as conceived of in this view, does not change significantly from day to day. This type of research searches the interior of the person's cognition and motives with the hope of discovering certainty. What this view is seriously lacking is a way to account for the relation people have with the social world and the process of human interaction and its formative capacity.

The traditional approach does not examine the complex and dynamic process of communication in use among people. Interaction is generally attributed to an internal psychic process further divided into cognitive and affective realms. The making of meaning is seen as an individual act and understanding is thought to exist in the mind of the person prior to action. Work is understood from the vantage of expectations and personal characteristics. Traditional methods of inquiry focus on individual preferences, psychological identification, cognitive consistency, and intrinsic motivations. Behavior is seen as the consequence of cognitive status and is reduced to the process of counting the occurrence of behavior elements. In fact, some of these researchers have provided a list of attributes (as indicated above) that describe universal features of workers with high work values, interests, and involvement. While such categorizations may have some utility in describing general common traits, they do not adequately explain the complexity of the meaning of work, or how the meaning of work and its role emerges among people in specific contexts. Work itself is being studied as a concrete entity that exists in universal attributes found in individuals. In this tradition, work is measured by a host of empirical facts. This reification does not consider the social aspects and influences of interpersonal relationships on shaping the meaning of work nor does it consider the multitude of differing contexts.

Sociological Perspective of Work

Work has also been studied from various sociological perspectives that posit that the workplace cannot be understood as a contained space apart from the larger social landscape. Epstein (1990) noted that survey research done mostly from the 1950s through the 1970s has focused on social-psychological attributes reported by workers without regard to context. Survey responses have been accepted as accurate without consideration of dynamics such as norms that determine certain answers to questions, or the fact that surveys limit the analysis to factors identified by questionnaires. As a result, little has been learned about the place of work in people's lives. Epstein stated that we have forgotten to ask what conceptions people hold about work, whether or how people identify with their jobs, and how the boundaries between the workplace and other spheres of life are experienced.

Sociologists have studied the workplace culture and have found that workers are active beings who endow the workplace with meanings and interact in the work setting in ways that reflect their larger world (e.g., Kimeldorf, 1985; Lamphere, 1985; Westwood, 1982). However, this research has mostly led to articulating the way workers view their work roles, and the creation of identity through work. The research has not addressed the reflexive relationships that exist among people.

Stinchcombe (1990) argued the workplace is governed by rules and norms that are found in the larger culture. This direction of research highlights the cultural influences on the experience of work. He saw that informal modes of discourse were mistakenly conceived of as matters of social organization when they are cultural. He noted there are often two sets of norms like different languages in the workplace (formal and informal discourse) and that experienced workers have the ability to use both in their work day. The formal discourse is reserved for issues such as technical matters, and the informal discourse is called upon when discussing personal or social matters. Stinchcombe noted the importance of informal modes of discourse in shaping the workplace. Another aspect of the larger culture that influences work is apparent in how work is assigned. Work assignments are influenced by social expectations placed on factors such as gender and race. Classifications of jobs are often related to classification of sex. For example, jobs that require nurturing of others, occur during the day, have low levels of danger, and require managing interpersonal relations are seen as jobs most appropriate to women. Jobs that are impersonal, are scheduled at night, have a high degree of danger, or require managing large sums of money are seen as jobs for males (Ortner, 1974). Stinchcombe's intent is to demonstrate that studying work as an abstraction is ineffective as the wider culture influences and shapes what happens as people interact and call upon cultural resources.

Critique of Sociological Approaches

A dominant theme of sociology has been the effect of work on the person, and much of the work of sociologists has attempted to show that work conditions influence the worker's personality. There are few studies that focus on the meaning of work itself. There is a wealth of information on the transformation of the physical nature of work in the past one hundred years, but there is not much research dedicated to the symbolic importance of work (Zuboff, 1983).

While the sociological view has some features that include factors such as cultural influences, it too has largely relied on empirical methods to make observations and posit a universal set of principles that describe work. Efforts by Stinchcombe placed greater emphasis on the communication process shared by individuals than the traditional approaches to understanding work, but generally have not explored the depth of the communication process.

These approaches to work have yielded vivid characterizations of what they have observed, and offered static predetermined explanations for behavior thought to be common to group members. The interest has been in producing empirical evidence to explain fundamental laws of human action and the individual interpretive process or operation of social forces on individuals (Cronen, Pearce, & Xi, 1989). However these studies have not understood or described the complexity and creativeness of interaction within situated encounters among people.

Research from the Field of Communication

There are many researchers who have provided a wealth of research about the communication practices of people within organizations. Once again the focus is on paid employment with a primary goal of understanding how organizations function. However, the literature within the field of communication about the meaning of working is limited. Mumby and Stohl (1996) describe research within the field focused on collective action, agency messages, symbols, and discourse with emphasis on central problematics of (a) the problematic of voice; (b) the problematic of rationality; (c) the problematic of organization; and (d) the problematic of the organization–society relationship. The research accounts for what they described as the complex and collaborative nature of communicating, organizing, and knowing.

Exploring the problematic of voice has produced research which may be the most relevant to this study. This research direction looks for the meaning systems people bring to the workplace and how meaning is made in communication. The research is directed toward finding the number of different voices within an organization that shape organizational knowledge. There are many studies that have included groups that have tended to be marginalized as making significant contributions to organizational knowledge. Among these studies, those that have included the role of women has led to new understanding of organizational life and the contributions of women to organizations (Buzzanell, 1994; Haslett, 1992; Mumby, 1992; Tannen, 1990; Wood, 1994). Mumby and Stohl (1996) identify other contributions that have been made by researchers who are concerned with the problematic of voice. Voices that have led to deeper understandings of organizational life include the voices of people of color, and the voices of workers and their strategies in getting managers to conform to their wishes. While much of the research in the field of organizational communication does not directly relate to the direction of this book, there are many common features that this vein of research shares with this study. The most salient of these are the concerns with the constitutive role of communication, reality as a social construction, and that communication is more than information transmission. Many organizational communication researchers share the belief that communication has multiple meanings, and is a primary aspect of social life. Communication is regarded as organic, creative, and dynamic (Cheney, 1995; Deetz, 1982; Mumby, 1988). These researchers have provided invaluable methodological approaches and findings to the field of communication. However, the theme of the research is most relevant to paid employment.

This book intends to explore working in all aspects of a person's life, which has led to using a philosophical position and methodology that would be flexible and capable of extending beyond the work setting and paid employment. In the following chapter the reader is introduced to American pragmatism and the Coordinated Management of Meaning as positions that offer a philosophical direction and methodology to explore the stories of working among the Acadian Americans.

Chapter 4

American Pragmatism and the Coordinated Management of Meaning

THIS CHAPTER PROVIDES a brief overview of American pragmatism and the Coordinated Management of Meaning (CMM) as a practical theory of communication. The philosophical position of pragmatism and the communication theory of CMM provide a lens for examining the ambiguity and the dynamic nature of concepts such as work, and as a method to analyze the stories the Acadian Americans related in the interviews. CMM is a methodology capable of entering into this culture and interpreting what is found there according to the tenets of American pragmatism.

The ambiguity of the term work, and the lack of agreement as to the most meaningful ways to comprehend it necessitate the use of a comprehensive and flexible approach to inquiry. Approaches that explore individual attitudes, uncover camouflaged psychological processes, or categorize social practices have not yielded a credible appreciation of the meaning of working itself. CMM, grounded in pragmatism, is offered as an effective methodology capable of investigating and explaining the multiple interests present, and the forces operating on people in communicative events. CMM regards communication as a coordinated action co-constructed by people participating in specific episodes. Communication is regarded as much more than a simple vehicle for message transmission. Using CMM provides a means to understand how social phenomena are created in the process of conjoint action, and it describes ways that participants in conversation are obliged to act and speak in certain ways. What the Acadian Americans have to say in interviews is informed by meanings that have been constructed by the members of their culture. Work, as with other concepts discussed in the interviews, has a significance that extends beyond the word itself. CMM, grounded in pragmatism, will help to reveal the significance of working, family, church, and the rules and forces for action that the Acadian Americans enact.

American Pragmatism

Pragmatism and CMM provide an alternative to the traditional perspective by regarding communication as a primary social process, and rejecting the notion of a fixed set of truths. Pragmatism's overarching goal has been to help people think in new ways and make connections to other ways of living their lives. The concern is with the present moment and its connection to the future while considering the context, participants and forces at work in each episode. Pragmatism was presented by Charles Saunders Peirce in the 1870s as a method for making ideas clear and a place to look for ideas. William James regarded pragmatism as a way of doing philosophy and as a theory of truth. John Dewey later developed and amplified Peirce's and James's contributions and constructed the bridge between science and human values. However, Dewey's contribution was far more than a synthesis of James and Peirce. Dewey expanded the possibilities for pragmatism, which will be discussed below. Lastly, George Herbert Mead developed a comprehensive theory of mind and behavior. The origins of pragmatism are not particularly clear.[1] James referred to it as a new name for some old ways of thinking (1907). Pragmatism appears at the end of the nineteenth century as a response to a host of problems in modern philosophy. James, in his work titled *Pragmatism,* saw pragmatism as a mediator to resolve the dilemma within philosophy. The dilemma places science on one side, and religious and moral values on the other. Pragmatism emerged to integrate these two separate domains of thought and action in modern philosophy. Thayer (1968) suggested that the ultimate purpose of pragmatism was moral. The purpose is moral in his view because pragmatism could render the meaning of ethical and metaphysical beliefs and decisions of conduct into terms that could be analyzed and verified by established norms of scientific judgment. Pragmatism thereby offered a theory of knowledge where knowing is an evaluative activity. Thayer saw two main phases in the development of pragmatism. The first phase was the forming of a maxim of meaning by Peirce and expanded upon by James, and the second phase was a more comprehensive development of a theory of inquiry, knowledge, and valuation influenced by Dewey.

The pragmatic concern is not with what we think, but how we think and act in a world we are active participants in. The need to open ourselves to new possibilities may be interpreted to mean there is something wrong with the way we live now. However the pragmatists shared the belief that the problems are not in people, but in the way people approach issues. It seems people are often confronted with puzzles and riddles of life. These challenges may dissolve if we have a new way of looking at them, or if we are freed from beliefs that confuse us. Pragmatism is not a mechanical method that once applied in all human situations we witness improvement. The application of pragmatism to real-life situations can provide people with the means to rethink and adjust to situations in new ways. A unique feature of pragmatism is that it does not make promises or claims to eradicate the puzzles of life. Pragmatists contend that there are no absolute truths to be discovered. Our actions are based on what we see the world as today, and what we anticipate it to be tomorrow. Dewey in particular offered a vision that did not rely on the familiar concepts of truth as offered by Hegel which saw philosophy as capable of knowing what is imperishable, eternal, and absolute (Hegel, 1975). Pragmatism's goal was to relieve philosophy's hold on humankind as the pathway to knowledge and truth. Pragmatism holds a future orientation and is emancipated from method and belief that seeks reason and truth as the basis of knowing.

Although the exact genesis of pragmatism is not clear, the history that precedes it can be explored. Prior to the development of pragmatism the Hegelian position was the dominant position in philosophy. The Hegelian view is the culmination of several centuries of philosophical trends as traced by Rorty (1979). Philosophy established itself as possessing a special understanding of the nature of knowledge and of the mind. Philosophers were active in denouncing claims to knowledge made by science or any discipline. Knowledge represented the cumulative assets of culture, and philosophy played a role in determining what is an accurate representation of knowing. It was commonly believed that knowing is the ability to accurately represent what is outside the mind; therefore under this premise knowing is the ability to understand how the mind produces or constructs these representations. Philosophy's task was to be the general theory of representation. Rorty attributed this philosophical position to the contributions of Descartes, Locke and Kant in constructing the idea of the mind as the subject of study. Descartes first provided the concept of mind as a separate and distinct entity. In the seventeenth century, Locke presented the theory that knowledge is based on an understanding of mental processes. Kant empowered philosophy as the judiciary of pure reason by giving it the capacity to accept or reject claims of what constitutes knowledge. The contributions of Descartes, Locke and Kant raised the mind as the central focus of attention, as the mind exists as an object of inner space consisting of elements that make knowledge possible. Philosophy and philosophizing are made foundational by these moves. Descartes' contribution is the transcendental method in modern philosophy where the mind determines certain conditions and effects in the objects known. Knowledge of the world is mediated by innate ideas. The method is an attempt to uncover what the mind and its ability contribute to our sensations of objects in order to produce knowledge. Derived from Plato's anamnesis, the soul possesses principles and vision of forms to make knowing possible. Thus, reasoning is the path to knowing. Locke and the empiricists believed that knowledge of the world was immediate. The mind is a blank slate that is altered as reality impresses itself upon it through the senses. Sense data thus becomes the building blocks of knowledge of the world.

Western Europe experienced profound changes in its culture influenced by the contributions of Cartesian logic, eighteenth century enlightenment, and the rise of science. Science challenged the foundation of older cultural values and ethical ideals. There was a pressing need to interpret moral experience, the meaning of science, and what constitutes knowledge. Kant addressed the conditions which account for science and at the same time discovered the assumptions that make moral experience possible. Kant brings together the two philosophical traditions of the time. He joins the empiricist position that ideas are perceptions grounded in sense experience with the rationalists' position that ideas are intelligible forms and acts of judgment (Thayer, 1968). The dilemma Kant faced was this: does knowledge result from rational principles, and if so was reason of primary importance, or did knowledge emanate from individual perceptions, and if so, is sense the primary process of knowing? Kant provided a third position which assimilates these views with the idea that reason functions to organize, interpret, and synthesize sense experience. Kant agrees there are no such things as innate ideas, but he does not see all knowledge as derived from experience. Kant reverses the empiricist's position and says that all experience must conform to knowledge rather than all knowledge must conform to experience. Kant "discovers" that the mind is an active agent in ordering and interpreting sense data. Kant's efforts rescued philosophy, and the mind remains in the primary position in the establishment of knowledge. Philosophy experiences other critical developments after Kant. Romanticism and modern idealism are two examples of the major shifts in philosophy. As Rorty explained, the nineteenth century was dominated by Hegel's philosophical contributions which stressed a monistic idealism that was committed to the belief that there was one mental substance, and reality and truth are the entire system in which all propositions are rationally connected. During this time economic and political expansion of nations, agricultural and industrial revolutions, and the Darwinian evolution served as the stimulus for profound changes in the world. The stage was set for the pragmatists to enter into the discourse of Western philosophy. The pragmatists could not ignore the social and political changes, and most importantly the major shifts in thinking brought about by evolutionary biology. These events compelled them to find new ways to make sense of the world.

The pragmatists raised objections to the foundational notion of philosophy. Pragmatism avoided the pitfalls of the traditional philosophers and chose not to debate the dominant ideas of the subject. The pragmatist's role was to emancipate people, and ultimately society as whole, from the power of mind as the center of knowledge and the power of pure reason. The pragmatists thought it was an error to allow philosophy to serve as a judge and jury of life. Pragmatism envisioned a different world made possible by integrating science with philosophy, and shifting philosophy to a practical art for living. Pragmatism looked beyond the internal world of the subject and looked outward to a world of action.

It was Peirce who offered pragmatism as a method of philosophizing about the theory of meaning, and as a method for achieving clarity of our ideas (Peirce, 1905). Peirce thought that the meaning of any statement is the procedure of its verification. His method of inquiry offered an alternative to the widely held belief that clear and distinct concepts serve as the foundation of knowledge. Peirce believed that the meanings of concepts are contextually based, and defining a meaning is dependent upon interests and conditions (Peirce & Buchler, 1940). Perhaps Peirce's most significant contribution is his view of the communal form verification takes on. Verification can only occur within a community of widely known system of procedures and beliefs, or what he regarded as a socially inherited system of knowledge (Peirce, Hartshorne & Weiss, 1931). Knowing is therefore not a private matter.

Williams James's (1912) goal was to remove the subject as the focus of debate, which was typical of philosophy and the logical positivist method. James saw a world that was ontologically open and dynamic, and in direct contradiction with a world that sought fixed truths and static principles. In *A Pluralistic Universe* (James, 1909) he expressed the idea that we live in an unfinished universe, and a world that is in the process of being made. Being alive in this universe is a dynamic process. We enter into the world with a living contemplation that keeps us open to experience and possibilities. A world that is in process of being made has multiple possibilities and cannot rely on static principles as each situation opens new ways of thinking and acting. James felt the focus should move from the intentions in the mind of the individual to the actions of people. In James's view the mind and consciousness are instruments that allow the person to act in the world. Consciousness is not a simple mosaic of events. It is a multiplicity of relations and events that make up experience. James described consciousness as a continuum of experience, and not fragments of unrelated events. He felt the traditional empiricist's position fails to see the continuity of experience, and the rationalists' positions failed to see the discontinuity of experience and instead calls upon the transcendent self and reason to overcome the uncertainty of the world. Pragmatism has a strong affinity with the concept of continuity which sees a world of no gaps, breaks, or cleavages. The pragmatists' concerns are with identifying growth, and development in all living things. This represents a significantly different way of making sense of experience such as work. Inquiry that regards concepts such as work as detached from social and individual life fails to overcome the subject/object dualism. This dualism does not hold up when people speak. Communication becomes an active agent calling upon agreed-on symbols and sounds to coordinate action with others in the environment.

Shusterman (1997) noted a shift in pragmatism as Dewey attempted to free philosophy from the search for foundations. Dewey did not see the fixed concepts such as the cogito, or *a priori* laws of thought as necessary or useful in understanding human practices. Dewey, in the pragmatist's tradition, sought ways to reform philosophy and redirect it to an art of living. Dewey extended James's ideas and emphasized the need for social theory that could enrich social life and resolve social and cultural issues. Philosophizing in Dewey's opinion can act to transform society, which is the converse of foundational philosophy. Dewey regarded philosophy as a civic enterprise. In *Philosophy and Civilization* he described philosophy's connection with social history, and with civilization as natural (Dewey, 1931).

This brief account of the rise of pragmatism will be helpful in identifying the central features of the Acadian–American stories.

Experience as a Central Feature of Living

Experience is an important concept in the philosophy of pragmatism. James spoke of experience as the continuum of parts that flow together and form a unity (James & Perry, 1912), and Mead shared Dewey's conception of experience as a confluence of persons' abilities and the phenomena of the world in situated action (Mead & Morris, 1934). However, experience takes on a much more central focus in Dewey's position. Dewey thought that experience describes the relationship between the individual, society, and institutions, and it expresses the unity of thought and action. While the traditionalists thought of experience as a subjective affair, separate and distinct from objective reality, Dewey saw experience as a part of the objective world, which enters into the actions of people and may be modified by a person's response. Experience is inclusive of all transactions and processes that the person encounters in living a life, and life itself is made up of a string of overlapping and interpenetrating experiences and situations. Dewey makes it clear that there is no conscious experience without inference, and reflection is an ongoing process that people use to make sense of events and act into the future (Dewey, 1976). The consequence of action provides a future orientation to the world as each action has a consequence and actors know there is more to this life than this moment (Dewey, 1925). People acting with awareness that there is a consequence to actions have a concern with a future and their active relationship with others. This awareness compels actors to communicate and call upon co-constructed means of acting. The mind is not an outside observer of the world. Instead, the mind is an active part of the world. Experience traverses the object–subject split as people are involved in transactions in communication and social life. Knowledge emerges from our interactions and the consequences (imagined or real) based upon a coordination of past, present and future. Dewey (1976) maintains that experience is not the equivalent of knowledge, but that "knowing is one mode of experiencing" (3:159). Experience is inclusive of peoples' continuous transactions with all of nature and through a process of inquiry people come to know the world around them.

Communication, Joint Action, and Knowing

Dewey (1916) observed that thought and action are presented in the western tradition as a duality, with mind and thought as favored. Yet in doing so we fail to see the complexity of experience, and that thought is a feature of action. Persons are always entering into patterns of activity with others and become who they are based upon their embodied actions that are coordinated with others (Cronen, 1995a). Coordinated action, or joint action between two or more people exemplifies how experience represents a unity of thought and action that is organized in a pattern of practice. Dewey's idea of experience as a unity of thought and action directs us to look for situated communication between people as the place to observe society. It is within the conjoint action that people make use of shared rules, which are enacted and reinforced through talk. Dewey referred to communication as a process of sharing experience until it becomes a common possession. This process of sharing experience modifies the people who participate in it (Dewey, 1916). Dewey (1922) saw a communal nature to experience and recognized that the thoughts of people are not theirs alone, but the result of interaction with others. This concept is valuable when studying the communication of members of a culture such as the Acadian Americans.

Dewey speaks directly of the process of communication when he recognizes that knowing cannot exist without communication. Dewey felt that knowing occurs in the process of doing, as meaning and knowledge arise in the process of doing and living in action with others (Cronen & Lang, 1994). Meaning is developed by participants through the conjoint action that people participate in together. Dewey saw communication playing a critical role as the primary social process. He felt that society's continuation exists in transmission, in communication (Dewey, 1916). Identity is not an innate feature but becomes constituted through the process of communication and our experience with the world. Language is regarded as a social necessity as people express needs, habits and desires; and language facilitates social life that forms the basis of who we are. The pragmatists, and more specifically Dewey, regard communication as a critical process of life.

Ends-in-View

Dewey's conception of ends-in-view has particular importance when exploring situated interaction. The end-in-view may be thought of as a projection that works as an instrument to accomplish the actual end or consequences. The end-in-view serves as a plan that accounts for events in the context, the desired state, and the projected consequences of actions. Dewey stated in his *Theory of Valuation*, "The end-in-view is that particular activity which operates as a coordinating factor of all sub-activities involved" (p. 234, Dewey, 1981). People call upon an end-in-view that will organize their experience and bring about a desired or acceptable end to their action. The end-in-view is not the outcome, although the actual outcome can be identical; it operates differently from the outcome itself. The end-in-view serves an important function as people attempt to resolve challenges. Through projecting ends-in-view, they are able to weigh the existing conditions in the present difficulties, the desired resolution of the issue, and the likely consequences for action. The ends-in-view serve as the plan to arrange possibilities for action into a process that brings about the desired or acceptable state.

Aesthetics and Consummatory Experience

Experience and action are informed by aesthetics of interaction. In *Art as Experience* (Dewey, 1934) aesthetic experience is described as a critical aspect of experience itself, and it is in the aesthetical dimensions that experience is the most complete. Dewey regarded each experience as having an immediacy that is directly felt. The aesthetic quality of experience holds the complex parts of an experience together, and it can guide the development of the experience. When an experience is filled with meaning, ideas, and emotion, it becomes restructured. Dewey referred to the restructured experience as a consummation. Aesthetics are always present, but experience does not always attain consummation, which may be understood as the moments where things achieve a fit. Dewey termed experiences that are characterized by completeness and intensity as consummatory experiences, which occur at many moments in the living of a life. There are the moments of satisfaction and fulfillment, or there can be those of disappointment. Emotions and consummatory experiences should not be discounted when explaining the meaning of events and actions in a person's life. This breaks with traditional ways of accounting for knowledge based upon only those things that can be observed. Dewey felt that knowing extends beyond essences or the universal, and there is a place for the immediacy and consummatory aspects of an experience. Consummatory experience is what Dewey saw as experience in its total richness as it includes knowing, suffering, envying, searching, and questioning (Dewey, 1981). Aesthetic experiences are significant in opening a person to new possibilities for experience. Feelings that people experience are part of the consequence at the moment of reflection. People know when things are "right" in the way feeling are organized to tell them the action was "done right." The person reflects on the feelings and weighs it against similar feelings or experiences and knows this is right. Such moments may lead to consummatory experience. This is a moment in living where things have a beautiful fit. These consummatory experiences are tied to larger cultural frames that define what are the beautiful moments or awkward moments of living. People learn through living in association what parts of experience are the most moving. Aesthetic experiences are important in informing a person of the consequences of their actions and what adaptations must be made to reach an end-in-view. A desired state is often associated with emotions that inform a person when it has or has not been achieved. People may restructure a problematic situation and initiate a course of action that will resolve the situation.

Aesthetics are a not a private matter, but they become what they are within the context of experience that is situated within a specific culture (Dewey, 1934). What constitutes a consummatory experience is defined by persons living within a culture; the prime source of meaning is found in the culture's rules and forces for action that must be satisfied and render an experience coherent. Following Dewey, Averill (1980) described emotions as emerging in coherent ways in patterns of social action, and roles are socially defined. These socially defined roles are important in telling a person how to act in particular contexts where they experience emotions. These emotional states or aesthetic experiences are not permanent states that people live in; they are transitory, and socially constructed.

The consummatory experiences are not knowledge, they are experiences that provide a qualitative immediacy that goes beyond what can be observed; they allow a different way to think and talk about communication. While sense impressions, attention, and perception are common ways to think of communication, consummatory experience allows us to explore how people learn a kind of joy or disappointment they derive from their actions. As Dewey (1938) described, there is a way that we connect to the world and there are aesthetic dimensions to all activity. Dewey and other pragmatists do not see the aesthetic dimensions of life as the opposite of practical skills and techniques. Dewey in particular recognizes the connection between consummatory experience and life's needs and interests. He and other pragmatists have looked for ways to integrate life with aesthetic experience to enhance living. Acadian Americans identified a common feeling of satisfaction when they accomplish a work task. This is described as an important and fulfilling—or what Dewey referred to as a consummatory—experience. This study explores the consummatory experiences of the participants to enhance understandings of the experience of working, and how working has become so central to the life the Acadian Americans live.

Instrumentalism

The development of pragmatism is often regarded as occurring in two distinct phases (Thayer, 1968; Shusterman, 1997; Putnam, 1995). The first phase is the formulation of the maxim by Peirce and the revival of Peirce's ideas by James. The second phase is the more comprehensive development of a theory of inquiry and knowledge by Dewey, Mead, and Lewis. Dewey's work was dedicated to developing a theory for intelligent action. Scientific facts and moral values were interpreted as instruments for enriching the quality of experience (Boydston, 1970). Much of Dewey's work was focused on how people come to know what they know, with thought and experience becoming necessities in living a life. Instrumentalism serves as a functional description of thought as a process that is contingent upon challenges in the environment that leads people to initiate a process of inquiry that will enrich their life (Dewey, 1938). Dewey's instrumentalism was directed at aspects of intelligent action as it anticipated the consequences of action. Regarding communication as instrumental in living a life is important for Dewey and this later phase of pragmatic thinking. Communication is instrumental because it enhances and creates experience, guides life, and develops opportunities for exchange of thought. Communication is a necessity to go on in making sense of the world. Consequences are measured by specific practical effects that may be observed in the community. Inquiry is a social activity that comes through social inheritance. Thus, inquiry has a social character.

The pragmatists' position initially stated by Peirce and James, and later widened by Dewey, leads to methods that accept the ideas of plurality, indefiniteness of all things, and a commonsense attitude toward every aspect of human experience. Just as evolutionary development never ceases, the pragmatists believe there is a changing world that awaits discovery and is filled with unlimited possibilities. CMM, a communication theory, is grounded in the philosophy of pragmatism and is presented here as theory and as a methodology to study the meaning of working for Acadian Americans.

The Coordinated Management of Meaning

CMM provides a practical theory that is grounded in the pragmatist's perspective, as well as the work of Ludwig Wittgenstein, and the work of Gregory Bateson. Continuing in the vein of work initiated by the pragmatists, CMM seeks alternatives to traditional approaches that see the world as static, and research that yields universal laws and fixed truths. CMM is capable of describing the real world and the situated actions of people engaged in interaction. CMM contends that it is in the process of communication that social life and individual experiences are created. Communication practices are social actions that create, and sustain social realities for participants in a given context. Pearce and Cronen (1980) offer an alternative to the western notion of communication which they saw represented as a linear process of sending and receiving messages. They conceived of communication as a form of action persons perform together in contexts with each other. Consistent with the pragmatists' views, reality is not fixed or certain. Instead, reality is created through the interactions of participants. Through the recursive process of interaction, participants reflect and in-turn change what they know and how they act in various situations. The individual, society, social practices, and institutions are defined as emerging from communication practices, rather than as fixed, separate entities that provide objective responses to particular needs (Pearce, 1989; Pearce & Cronen, 1980). CMM contends that a communication theory should be able to help us answer the basic questions of who we are, what it is to live a life, and how the process of communication contributes to living (Cronen et al., 1988). CMM can provide a method for inquiry that has the capability of addressing the ambiguities in the meaning of work

A critical aspect of CMM is that meaning, structure, and action. as well as individuality and association, arise in the reflexive relationship among these concepts. The patterns of social life come from the reciprocal production and interaction of individual and societal resources. These produce a forming coordination of the individual's resources such as consciousness, emotion, mental activity, and intention with societal resources, which includes physical environment, and social institutions. A forming coordination shows that thinking is not separate from interaction. The interactions people have with others form what they know, and how they know. It may be said that knowing turns back on the interaction (Cronen, 1995b). This forming coordination creates and sustains the social reality that the participants live within.

Communication does not represent an objective world. Words, languages and their meanings have an equivocal nature which allows a world of multiple meanings and possibilities. This imperfection of communication generates countless ways of living. Within this framework the researcher enters into a system and explores the rules and grammars that are at work for the members for the system to understand their meanings and actions.

CMM is in sharp contrast to positivist theories that exhort a philosophy of language, and envision the universality of underlying meaning and intentions of individual utterances. CMM makes no such claims nor attempts to suggest such conditions of certainty (Cronen et al., 1989). Conversation is regarded as the unit of observation, and participants' interactions in episodes as the unit of analysis. Within these episodes, CMM describes the imperfection and dynamical nature of communication. Imperfection and the unfinished nature of communication are not regarded as failings. Instead these are embraced as strengths of the human experience which recognizes that communication is a part of an evolving human condition. As meaning arises in action, we see that meaning is never finished, which opens possibilities for people in their ways of interacting with each other. Thinking of communication in this way is consistent with an evolutionary point of view that Cronen (2000b) described as a perspective that observes the way one event enters into the nature of the next and how that opens and closes possibilities for the future. The ongoing process of interaction leads to multiple directions that are not predictable, or reducible to universal concepts.

Communication is viewed as formative, meaning who we are is a compilation of experience and interactions with others. CMM contends there are few, if any innate features defining who we are. Rather, it is through processes of interaction with others that we are constituted. The impact of conjoint action shapes who we are. What people do together constitutes conjoint action, and the actions of individuals are influenced by their own interests and desires as well as the actions of those around them (Shotter, 1984). When we act into the action of others, we coordinate our thoughts and actions in a unity to attain coherence with other members in our social world. CMM regards language and communication as social as opposed to a simple set of symbols that people call upon to associate with each other. Volosinov (1976/1927) stated that "every utterance is the product of the interaction between speakers and the product of the broader context of the whole complex social situation in which the utterance emerges" (p. 79). The social aspects of interaction have a profound impact on who we are. CMM is a communication theory that provides us with a way to view social interaction as a primary source of who we are and how people live a life in and through communication.

Language Games, Grammar, and Levels of Context

Wittgenstein (1958) described "language games" as apparent in the practice of language as one person calls out the words and the other acts on them. A language game is "language and the actions into which it is woven" (7). Following Wittgenstein, "a meaning of a word is a kind of employment of it. For it is what we learn when the word is incorporated into our language" (1969). Terms can have different meanings among different groups of people. The grammar of a term includes the rules that help the members to make sense of the meaning of words and the actions associated with it. Rules and grammar inform the members how to act with others. Grammar, in the Wittgensteinian sense, is not limited to words; it is extended to concepts and actions. Therefore, making sense of a word or concept is more than an ability to recognize it. Understanding is the capability to act according to patterns of action that have developed in situated practice. In an episode of interaction the grammar of the conversation includes the way that people coordinate their feelings and actions in a way that they can continue the conversation in a meaningful way. Wittgenstein's ideas about language as the weaving of words with actions and rules is consistent with the discussion of Cronen's concept that life is created in the process of communication.

Action arises within levels of context that are hierarchically arranged and reflexive. Each level of context has its own logic of meaning and action. Patterns of practice emerge from five different, but related contexts of levels of action which includes: (1) self: how people identify themselves under particular conditions, (2) culture: the set of actions enacted by a group of people that are similarly patterned in their use of individual and social resources, (3) episodes: the specifically structured and bounded sequences of conversational actions, (4) interpersonal relationships: which denote the patterns between people and objects and their reflexive effects on each other, and (5) speech acts: the language used in a particular situation that leads to particular meanings within that situation (Pearce, 1994). Within a moment of conversation the primary level of context will act as the context for all other levels, and it provides the grammar for deciding action. A hierarchical ordering of the levels of context is not static and it adapts to the directions of the interaction.

Stories as a Feature of Communication

A cornerstone of CMM is exploring the stories people tell about who they are, would like to be, and exploring what stories people live within episodes of human action. Cronen (1994) claims people have many stories about their relationships, and ways to enact episodes that they draw upon to participate in conversations. The coherence of peoples' stories reflects their individual interpretation of the world. Our interactions with others are made up of the stories we tell about who we are, and the stories we live, or those we create in action with others. How stories are coordinated can vary, but it is done in ways that present stories as expedient, desirable, and reflective of what each person considers good in life (Pearce, 1989). There are many possibilities for the stories people construct, or how the stories are coordinated with others. The coherence of a story is judged by its bearing and integration with other people in the context. In spite of the endless variety of stories, communication is possible at some level. There are no universal contexts that people live within because the contexts have been uniquely constructed by the social interaction of the people in the context itself. Stories do not follow a logical order, but the stories do contain connections between the members and connections to the past and the future. The researcher's task is to discover the relationship between the stories among the members of the system to find how the stories fit together in a hierarchy. The hierarchy as described by Tomm (1987) is a self-referential network that the person calls upon. The hierarchy is not fixed, and it is susceptible to change as the context shifts. Although the stories are not fixed, they do have an order. A higher-order story is one that is not likely to be affected by changes in other stories in the hierarchy. The lower-order story does not have effect on the story of the higher order directly. The levels of contexts are hierarchically arranged and reflexive with each level having its own logic of meaning, action, connections, and influence on the other levels. How the stories are connected tells people at what level the responses should be made. The higher order serves as the context for all the other levels and provides the knowledge or "grammar" for deciding what should be done in specific moments in a conversation. The higher ordered story, and the grammars available at various levels of context, may limit or strengthen the responses people can or should make.

In some stories the levels of context do not exist as a hierarchy, and loops are present that cause ambiguity in interaction. A *charmed loop* occurs when the system appears to be stuck in a relatively static pattern of behavior; it locks the system into a way of acting that is regarded as pleasant. In the case of a charmed loop, two alternative interpretations of one action exist simultaneously. Tomm (1988) described charmed loops as a reflexive process in which reversals in meaning remain basically the same. *Strange loops* exist when the stories have exclusive alternatives. The strange loops call upon an opposite rule. For example, an addicted person who achieves sobriety may think they are non-addicted, which reinitiates the abuse of the substance. Unlike the charmed loops here a reversal of levels results in a major change of meaning.

Telling a Story from a Person Position

A speaker in an interaction tells, or lives a story from a specific position. The position is determined by the speaker's understanding of events in the interaction. Each position brings with it a different thoughts and actions. When a speaker interacts from the first person position, they are focused on their individuality along with the concern at that moment. First person position may also include speaking about a group of persons and their characteristics. The second person position describes the person being spoken to, who may become the first person when responding to the person speaking. The third person position may be deemed the position of objectivity and is usually respected within Western modes of speaking. It can represent a voice of authority. A person in the third position observes and comments on action from a place outside of the interaction.

The Significance of Grammar, Morals, and Logical Forces

Cronen (1995b) asserted that people are born into already established and functioning social worlds. Competence in social worlds requires that people must learn the actions and rules of the existing practices in that world. Conversations contain the patterns and rules that have developed as part of living. The grammar of a practice contains the rules, or logical forces that guide and direct what can occur, or what is not allowed within an episode of interaction. These moral forces influence what people can and cannot do, and must or must not do. CMM is concerned with rules and how they constitute a moral order and are necessary to achieve coherence in human action (Cronen, 1991). CMM is consistent with pragmatism, which considered morals among its chief concerns. A goal for pragmatism and for CMM is addressing the moral issues people encounter. The purpose of study and research is to address moral concerns and lead people to a good life.

Deontic operators divided into two categories affect communication. The first category of deontic operators is those that people would have made a conscious choice to utilize in a given situation. These include responses that are legitimate, prohibited, obligatory, or undetermined. The person chooses actions based upon the responses that are appropriate and guided by the rules of social life. The second category of deontic operators represents responses that the actor would regard as having been caused by another person or event in the episode. These deontic operators may be caused, probable, random, and blocked. In these instances the individual regards their behavior as caused and out of their control.

People make choices about what should or should not be done and provide reasons an action has taken place. These actions and reasons are moral statements, or moral accounts of human action as they designate the conditions under which people are held responsible. The rules that direct human action emerge in the process of interaction, rather than singularly in the mind of an individual. In light of the importance of knowing and following social rules, CMM contends that communication is a moral matter. Coherence is contingent upon rules that guide a unity of self with interaction. Consequence is a prominent feature of CMM as it accounts for the responsive action people seek to elicit through interaction with others. The structure of rules directs our actions and the rules are known to us through practice. The structure of action influences acceptable practice, and practice is guided by the actions that are coherent to the members of a system. As Cronen explained, in conversation moral choices are made, or moral accounts are given, therefore moral communities are created through communication.

There are four forces beyond the deontic operators that have the capacity to affect the moral nature of interaction. These are the prefigurative forces, practical forces, reflexive needs, and reflexive effects. The prefigurative forces are the extent that the act and antecedent of another person influence or constrain how a person acts in conversation. Practical forces represent the extent that action is influenced by the consequences the person desires. Although in some instances people may act without regard for the consequences because of the strength of the force. Reflexive need is the need for a particular response from another person to sustain or extend the story. Reflexive effects describe the influences of action on structure whether the actions taken were those desired by the actors (Cronen et al., 1989).

Reflexivity has particular significance for CMM theory as it explains the impact of conjoint action. Our interactions are affected by the circular process that exists between actors in a given context. What is said influences the relation that exists between two actors, and the content of what is said influences the meaning of their relationship. Recognizing that it is a reflexive process among the members of a system that guides practice, the researcher is freed from exploring the intersubjectivity of individuals or uncovering the psychological processes. Understanding the actions of actors is not contingent upon looking inside people. Understanding is based upon the actions and patterns of interactions that people share. Through this process of reflexivity we see that thinking does not exist independent of language. Thinking is part of a language game and language becomes the central feature of thinking.

CMM a Practical Theory

CMM is referred to as a practical theory because it functions as a heuristic for exploring social interaction and provides a way to join in with the grammars of people and thus explore their patterns of action. Cronen has noted that practical theory is informed by data created in the process of engagement with others (Cronen, 2000a). CMM provides a functional way to examine the developing logic of meaning and action created by people through a process of conjoint action. CMM is able to explore the complex hierarchy of levels of meaning, the forces that bear on action in conversation, and the positioning of the participants. CMM offers a method for studying the way people act in the real world to create patterns of practice and forms of life. It allows the researcher to explore the grammar of conversational practice, which describes the organization of feelings, utterances, behavior and objects so that members in a system know how to act. CMM provides procedures to examine how practices themselves constitute a family of methods for studying situated social action and the ability to describe, explain, critique, and change social action. Lastly, CMM recognizes the co-evolution of consequences when practice and theoretical study are combined (Cronen, 1995b). This may be realized when CMM can assist the people in a study with finding new ways to live richer lives.[2]

The intent of this study is to explore the meaning of the grammar of working among Acadian Americans and how their social practices are created in and by communication. Therefore, CMM provides a comprehensive approach that will examine the numerous forces, rules, and practices present in episodes of interaction. CMM should be able to interpret the meanings that are informing the Acadian Americans' actions in conversations and lead to a far-reaching understanding of the grammar of working. CMM provides an adaptable methodology that focuses on the communication practices of people.

CMM allows a different way to approach the concept of working. This study enters into the grammar of working and provides an account of conjoint action that produces an understanding of the term working held by members of this community. In addition, CMM allows the study to explore the aesthetical dimensions and the consummatory experiences that occurred in working. This is a critical aspect of the Acadian Americans' experience. As a practical theory, CMM describes the features of discourse and provides a method for the study of social praxis and action (Cronen, 1995b). CMM as a practical theory generates useful interpretations, explanation, and critiques of situated human action. CMM is referred to as a practical theory because it allows the researcher to explore and make sense of discourse between people, and it provides a means for researchers to join in the activity of people in situated encounters. Episodes of conversation contain the rules people call upon to guide their actions, and the rules used to arrive at coherence. Therefore, data is found in episodes of conversation in various contexts, and these episodes reveal the practices of human activity. Consistent with Dewey's conception, experience describes the unity of mind and action contained in all of our practices. This methodology explores the experiences through the observation and analysis of conversation and episodes.

CMM as a methodology allows the researcher to move beyond the commonly held perspective of communication as a simple sender–receiver model. Within CMM communication is regarded as the primary social process and action that persons perform together in a specific context (Pearce & Cronen, 1980). In so doing, CMM was used to analyze the grammars of working, the place of working in living an Acadian-American story, and how stories and grammars of working guided their actions. The analysis focused on the moral orders and logical forces in the interaction among the members, and the stories they lived and told about working. Communication was analyzed as a constitutive force which creates, sustains, and modifies the grammar of working.

CMM and Circular Questions

The CMM analysis begins by locating selected conversational triplets and analyzes these to determine the logic of meaning and action. Changsheng (1991) described conversational triplets occuring in conversation, with each line serving as the antecedent, act, and consequence of the lines around it. Knowing the meaning of an utterance or action requires that we know the preceding and following actions. The conversational triplet can reveal the antecedents, the prior messages used to interpret the present action; the acts, the utterances or analogic action; and consequences which refer to the responsive action desired which may or may not be known or produced. These conversation triplets were used to identify the antecedents, acts and consequences that the members presented. The analysis showed the hierarchy of levels of contexts, the grammars, moral orders, and logical forces that shape the conversational action.

A CMM analysis is concerned with the hierarchy of stories to determine the relationships among the participants. The analysis focuses on the logical forces of conversation that show how interaction echoed the reflexive needs of the members as the episodes progressed. A CMM analysis also seeks to identify the moral order and deontic operators which guide the participants' interactions. This has particular importance for the Acadian Americans, as will be shown in the study. The events in an episode prefigure future action, but the action cannot be known because of the multiple possibilities that exist in a situated encounter.

While CMM is the method used for analysis, circular questioning is the method that was employed in conducting the interviews with the Acadian Americans. Circular questioning is a means to collect data about their experiences and CMM was used to organize and analyze the data. Circular questions differ from other forms of interviewing in significant ways. At the very core of the concept of circular questioning is the idea that there are connections among people within a system, such as a family, or organization, and a connection between the interviewer and the individuals. The researcher/interviewer conducts the inquiry on the basis of feedback from the participants in response to the information that has been solicited about the relationship or interactive patterns. Circular questioning sounds like real conversation with each response of the respondent followed by a question by the interviewer, though Tomm (1987) has pointed out that it is not real conversation. The interviewer has a purpose, which is to gather information and promote new ways of thinking for the participants. Circular questioning is often associated with the Milan Group[3] who experimented with new ways of making sense of behavior and communication through circular questioning. Gregory Bateson's *Steps to an Ecology of the Mind* (1972) influenced the thinking of the Milan Group. Bateson's ideas offered an alternative to the concept of homeostasis, and replaced it with differences between the levels of action and the levels of meaning within a system. This view represents a shift from a linear orientation to a systems orientation. Interaction among members of a system exceeds simple cause-and-effect relationships, and is regarded as a process of conjoint action that operates in a recursive manner among members of the system. Circular questioning accounts for different ways of working and exploring the communication among members of a system. Communication is not a vehicle for the exchange of ideas, but an essential feature of living, a complex interactive process that generates, sus-

tains, or changes meaning among members of a system through recursive interaction. As stated above, conversations and episodes are the primary points of
observation and analysis. The exploration of conversations and the features of
episodes may reveal the meaning for the members of a system.

The application of circular questioning is not limited to therapeutic contexts. Essentially, circular questioning is applicable to all settings where people
live and work. It is the relationships among people that is circular in terms of its
recursiveness. According to Cronen and Lang (1994), to say that we live in and
by communication is to claim that all living is done in relations with others, and
living is action dependent upon others. Cronen and Lang (1996) discussed the
essential features of what makes circular questions circular. They found that circular questioning allows the researcher to explore the grammar used by the
members of a system to determine the specific connection of meaning and
how the grammar of the system is organized. In fact, interviewers call on the
actual grammar used by the participants to enter into the system of meaning
and explore what rules are at work. Circular questions connect the participants
with episodes of interaction by asking questions like *"who is most concerned"?* or
questions that explore the sequences of events within an episode such as *"what
happens next?"* Circular questions are concerned with the circularity of time as
the researcher explores how the past and future relate to the present. Cronen
and Lang feel each utterance is connected to past, present, and future. Circular
questions explore the connection across stories by asking what other events and
actions are going on in the lives of the members of a system. In a circular interview the researcher will pay attention to the position people hold within an
episode. Position is a way of describing the relationship people have in the
interaction and discourse. Participants may speak from various positions within
a context. The positions refer to the social positions people hold within an
episode, or those that are socially assigned, such as "parent" or "supervisor." Circular questioning also sanctions the interviewer to pose questions to members
in a group about comments or actions of others. This is referred to as "gossiping in front of others." Gossiping in front of others is a way that the researcher
may generate information by asking other members within the system to comment on another member, or by calling on a co-interviewer to share ideas.

There are a number of general questions that may be asked in an interview
when using CMM. Foley (1999) identified a number of general questions that
are appropriate in conducting a CMM analysis. These general questions may
include: Which stories are prominent in the action? How are they accomplished? What are the relationships between the participants in the episode?
How is this episode punctuated and organized? What grammars of action and
grammatical abilities are present? How do the participants join, maintain, or
change the action? How do logical forces guide the flow and content of conversation? What are the reflexive needs of the participants and how are they

affirmed or not? What language games are present? What patterns emerge in each conversation and across conversations? What are the values and ethics of the stories, sequences, and actions? These general questions helped to focus the analysis of the data the members presented.

CMM searches to find the hierarchical arrangement of stories. How the stories fit together, as well as the levels of context as discussed in chapter 2 are significant to the interviewer. The multiple levels of context are used to explore the way the stories are enacted in everyday life. Because the hierarchy of stories is not dependent on logic, the hierarchical arrangement may change in the course of experience.

CMM offers a way to explore the unified process of experience by making sense of the reflexivity that goes on between members of system, and to distinguish how the episode is punctuated. The stories gathered through circular questioning and analyzed with the framework of CMM can reveal the coherence members of a system share. CMM is not used to reveal hidden laws of human nature; it is a means to describe and interpret communication. CMM as a research methodology extricates the researcher from judgment, and provides the researcher with a way to intelligently join in the activity of others so that it may be understood (Cronen, 1994).

PART TWO

The Stories of Work, Communion, and Selfhood

Chapter 5

Stories of Family Life and Work

AT THE OUTSET OF THE INTERVIEWS the participants identified family as the primary reason for working hard, both at home and at a job. The stories of family life and work illustrate episodes of action that follow consistent rules and moral orders. The shared stories were coherent to all of the participants, and the discussion that followed often extended the original story by relating similar stories that took place within another person's family. Although the organization of this section begins with family life, the analysis revealed there are no distinctions between family life, culture, religious belief, and work. A critical feature of Acadian-American life was revealed when the interviews explored the conception of the family. The grammars of work and family are entwined as well as the grammars of family and culture, and family and church. Acadian Americans cannot talk of culture without talking about their family, work, or church. Culture is lived within a family and these concepts cannot be separated because they do not differ. Work is also a feature of family life because of a deep cultural integration with family life. In order to enact an Acadian-American story of selfhood a person must work, and work in particular ways. Religious belief, which was enacted through participation in the church, is another major part of this integration. At times their actions mirror the practices within their religion of Roman Catholicism. Within most cultures, culture is talked of as a higher-level context that informs a family; people might say, this is how we are, and then, this is our culture; but this does not happen with the Acadian Americans. Acadian Americans do not tell stories that distinguish between our family, culture, or religion. The stories they tell are about families organizing experience into stories of family-culture, family-work, and family-church. There were no stories where families are distinct from the culture itself. The stories about family and culture tell you how to enact particular relationships. They tell you how to relate to your wife or husband, boss, children, neighbors, non-Acadians, and all others you interact with. For ease of reference the inseparable entity of family, culture, work, church will be referred to as FCWc. The findings presented in this chapter should clarify how these intertwined concepts act as one common feature of Acadian life.

Episodes of family stories demonstrate individuals acting within the context of an autobiography of "doing all you can do for your family"—what work roles a parent takes on, how families teach the concepts found in FCWc, and how parents teach their children to work hard.

Work at home is no different from work at a job, given the inseparable nature of FCWc. Distinctions are not made between work in these two settings because of the integration of work with all aspects of life. Acadian Americans experience moral forces that compel them to work in specific ways, and they must work in these ways for their family and to reaffirm their culture and selfhood. As will be illustrated in the following, an Acadian American works to accomplish tasks, provide for family, and to satisfy forces within the family and cultural rules and moral orders.

All of the interviews began by asking the question, "What do you think of when you hear the term *work*?" The initial responses described work at job settings and work at home, but soon within the interviews all groups spoke of work as something that has to be done to take care of your family. This includes work done at home, and jobs held outside of the home. Taking care of your family was done in much the same way for the past generation, and continues as a force for these participants in present-day life. The stories of their parents are important in telling these people what they must or must not do. The stories of familial relationships are important to Acadian Americans due to the high value placed on family life. The logical order for action has an association with the past where they developed the rules for action, and strong prefigurative forces were developed. However, the Acadian Americans in these interviews are actively engaged in extending the stories into present contexts.

There are multiple stories about their fathers who would work more than one job, or less than desirable jobs to provide for the family. There are also many stories about mothers working hard at housekeeping tasks. Below is an excerpt from a transcript talking about mothers, and what work in the home was like. This interview was held with a group of professionals between the ages of thirty-nine to forty-eight. All of these members were married, attended college or a professional school, and had families of at least one child. They are referred to in the remainder of the chapter as Group 1.

In the transcripts there are symbols that indicate unusual occurrences in the participants talk. Whenever the reader sees the symbol "[" this indicates an interruption. Words in all capitals indicates raising of the voice, underlining indicates emphasis, and :: indicates slowly pronouncing the word for emphasis. Lags in time are indicated by the length of time in parentheses.[1]

LINDA: Very long days with very hard work. Yep.

DORIS: Very long days and a [lot of

LINDA: [Growing up it was only the mothers working in the home. Housework was hard. We didn't have hot water. We had a wood stove and doing the wash by the wringer. My mother would start at 6 in the morning and stop at eleven at night. I remember her hands she would hang out the clothes in the cold COLD weather and she would have chapped hands.

DORIS: I remember mom having a wash board and she wanted our socks to be white and our underwear to be white and she would have, like, bubbles and blisters from scrubbing on that washboard.

The stories of mothers working hard doing laundry, preparing meals, and doing other housework tasks were common to all of the groups. The groups reported that mothers seldom sat down to relax. The participants said that it was common for their mothers to continue to work at ironing or sewing in the same room with family members who were watching television or doing other leisure time activities. The members reported that their mothers never stopped. The major features found in all the stories about working hard were parents that never complained about work, lack of money, or difficult situations. Their parents were constantly working at home or outside of the house. These features are discussed again as a characteristic of "motivated people." Members used the term "motivated people" to describe hard-working people, and among the features of motivated people is that they never complain. Mothers were described as working hard because of their commitment to their families, and never complaining about the amount of work they had to do.

Here are two small sections of transcript talking about fathers and the importance of working for family life. The first section is taken from the professional group described above, and the second section came from a nonprofessional group. The nonprofessional group was made up of four participants who ranged in age from forty-one to fifty years of age. All but one of the members worked in a factory, and the one member who did not work in a factory worked as a supervisor in a computer service firm. This group will be referred to as Group 2.

DORIS: My father had two jobs and all the time we were growing up my father never had one job he always had two jobs.

LINDA: My father would work all week in the factory at Simplex and then take the weekend watchman's job after he would work all week so we would have the basic things we needed.

JOAN: Dad would come home then he would go to his second job.

THERESA: We didn't have a lot of money, (3 seconds) now as far as I was concerned as a child I thought we had everything we wanted

((gap))

DORIS: <u>Everything</u> we wanted!

A second transcript from the nonprofessional group where two members are talking about Acadian men:

JOSEPH: Those guys would do whatever it took to put food on the table. Worked as lumberjacks in Canada, then wood shops here, which beat the hell out of working in the cold. Pretty much every father in my neighborhood had another job at night or on the weekend. Working for small money, lots of hours, never complain. Keep the family fed, clothed, and happy

CHARLES: That's right, my father, too. It was like that for all of us.

It was common for fathers to have more than one job in Acadian-American families. Most group members said this was out of necessity due to the low wages in the mills where most Acadians were employed. Fathers worked these second jobs, and in some cases a third job, to provide for their families. Although there was little money, there are stories of having everything you wanted as a child, as indicated above. However in others parts of the interviews, participants pointed out that they lived simply. All of these participants were children in the 1960s, which serves as a point of reference to lives they lived. They were clear that as children they did not have the number of toys or the opportunities other children had; only two reported owning a bicycle. Group members stated that there wasn't money for dance lessons, skiing at the nearby ski mountain, or to participate in other kinds of activities that other children in the city did. Having everything you wanted can be assumed to mean that your family provided food, clothing, and other basic items. However, the groups stressed how proud parents were of their children, and that they dressed them as well as they could afford for church on Sunday. Many times in the interviews members stated that living as an Acadian American you must not complain, and you make the best out of what life has given you. Not complaining and making the best of life refers to where you live, and work. It is possible that saying you have everything you needed, but not as much as others, is one way of stating differences without complaining. Saying we had everything we wanted may be the result of living in a way to make the best out of what you did have, and shows appreciation for what you were provided with.

The Primacy of Parenting-Work

The stories and strong moral orders are enacted in the current generation as well. While the sections of the transcripts highlighted above are referencing life as a child, there are many stories of present-day life that reveal the same degree of obligation to family. Parents have a strong obligation to provide for their children, and there are expectations for the parents to ensure their children's development as hard-working people. Parents were described as being stern, and disciplinarians who followed the same rules as those being taught in the parochial school and church, which is consistent with the FCWc dynamic. Later in this chapter the importance of religion is discussed, including enrollment in the church-supported elementary school. All of the groups reported that a close relationship existed between the church, school, and home. In the interviews all of the group members were asked, what kinds of stories do you tell your children about work? The participants reported that they teach by example, and frequently point out that things they have such as cars, a home, and vacations are only possible through hard work. All of the participants stated there are frequent discussions with their children about working hard. The members felt it is important to discuss work often with your children.

In the following section from a transcript the participants were asked a reflexive question about what would it be like if their children did not have the same work ethic. The response was emphatic.

MARIE: (makes a loud noise and laughs) that would be a tough one. I can't, I can't, I can't even think of that. They can't just shift from one job to another, they just can't.

CLAIRE: I would die. I come from a family where you work hard, even my husband's side does and they are not Acadian. He has these relatives that have gone through a hard time because their daughter quit college, ran off with a guy, and had a baby. Now they roam the countryside in a tent, and their son is not good either. My kids keep saying that I lecture, but I don't. If they got married right out of high school, I don't know the situation would be awful for them and their parents. God that scares me to think that could happen to my youngest. My oldest is all set now, married, a good job. My expectations are high.

As can be seen in this brief section of the transcript members talk about high expectations and that what children do with their lives is a matter of concern for Acadian-American parents. The discussion continued about the expectations parents had that their children should go to college, or be trained in a trade. The professional group was clear that they did not want their children to work in a factory as their parents had. The nonprofessional group expressed that they did not wish for their children to work in a factory, but that it was acceptable as long as the children were happy and could provide for their families. Even though all of the participants' fathers had worked in factories when they immigrated to the United States, there was opposition to their children working in factories. The professional group stated they had come too far to go back to factory work. All of the groups agreed that work in the trades was better than factory work because the pay is better, and a trade demands more skill. One member spoke proudly of his twin boys who work as sheet-rockers on weekends, and that the owner of the business stated they were his best workers. These two boys will work there full-time when they graduate from high school this spring. The member stated he saw this as a good start for them, because it is honest work. The other group members indicated that this was good and he and his wife must be proud of these boys.

As families teach their children about working a common story was revealed that children are taught to "do it for yourself." This term has a grammar of its own. In this case a mother stated that she tells her son to be proud for yourself when you so something well such as a good grade in school. She stated that she goes on to say, "don't do it for me, do it for yourself." Doing it for yourself becomes a way to get a sense of who you are, and it is a way that you are fulfilled through working. In a concept such as doing it for yourself the strong forces in the FCWc dynamic contribute to selfhood.

One of the participants in the interview proudly spoke of her "Acadian daughter" who is away at college on a scholarship, and is ranked at the top of her sophomore class. Her mother called her on a Saturday night while she was at school, and her daughter was in her dormitory studying while all her friends went out to eat. Her mother proudly pointed to this story as an example of the strong work ethic found in her culture and this was something her daughter learned at home. This episode may be regarded as her daughter living an Acadian-American story of working hard at all times, and doing this for herself. While other students are out a Saturday night, this young woman was moved by prefigurative forces that influenced a choice to work. There is a force informing her that she should be working. The mother talked about how she had always worked at teaching her children the importance of working hard. The mother's time and dedication to teaching her children how to live an Acadian-American story had a strong practical force. The mother acts in this way to help her children fit into the community as defined by the FCWc. The story also reveals the reflexive effective for the mother, as her daughter's success in school and athletics affirms her actions as an Acadian-American parent.

Doing it for yourself is also a strong reflexive force that informs an Acadian American that successful enactment is found in what you are about; it is not found in the job itself. This story is reinforced by working hard and finding pride in how work is done, no matter what the task. Doing it for yourself is not in contradiction within an inseparable FCWc system. There are features of this episode that are reminiscent of the concept of *altercasting* as employed by symbolic interactionists (Weinstein & Deutschberger, 1963). Briefly, altercasting occurs when we influence people's actions and cast them into a role we want for them. The person thinks of themselves and behaves in a manner that we or our culture wants. In this case, the familial-cultural definition of doing it for your self as a hard-working person influences how the person defines self. The college student begins to recognize herself in relation to others in her family/culture, and she acts in a way that is consistent with the label or conception. The ideas of doing it for yourself and working hard define this action as real. The college student takes action according to this label and acts as FCWc has directed, and by doing so she fulfills the definition, much like altercasting. This is not to say that all people within a culture or a family live to definitions and labels that have been constructed. CMM recognizes that people can construct multiple stories of their lives, and it is not a given that people conform to definitions. People can fail to conform to these definitions and in so doing create new definitions and possibilities. The student's actions may have been influenced by her Acadian-American FCWc story. She was cast into a role that the family desired and she began to think and act in a way that was expected. Doing it for yourself and working hard are not contradictory within this FCWc system because the casting influences selfhood and action. A person by acting an Acadian-American story is doing it for themselves and satisfying both selfhood and forces in FCWc.

Doing it for yourself has its foundations in a long-enduring story of hardships Acadians have experienced. Historically the adversities began in the eighteenth century and continued to recent times. Initially there was the diaspora of Acadians, one hundred years of isolation in New Brunswick, and then the migration to the United States because of economic deterioration. All of these events are filled with great difficulties. Emigration to the states did not end the hard times for Acadians. They worked at menial jobs and worked more than one job to support their families.[2] Later, in the 1970s, the mills shut down and the majority of the Acadians lost their jobs. They went to jobs that paid even less, but they made ends meet, and continued to work hard and provide for their families. Yet the stories these members relate are about parents who never complained, and families and a culture that can make the best of situations. Working hard, and having pride means that you endure difficult times. Many of the members talked about this ability to make the best of a situation as necessary to living your life, and part of being a hard-working person.

CHARLIE: I have learned to be pretty satisfied with my job. I have been there for over twenty years. My father would stay with a job, put in a hard day, long days, for many years. The shop closed up on him. I guess that happened to most of our dads. You can't look back. You move onto the next job. Work hard. Put bread on the table, and feel good about what you are doing. It all works out when you try and you will feel good when it does.

CLAIRE: You don't sit around and cry about things, you move on. My father would not say much, but when the plant he worked at closed he said to us we will be all right. I have two hands and I am not afraid to work. That will get us through this. I respected that. Sure enough we were back on our feet in no time[

MARIE: [Same thing in my family. You can come out on top if you work at it.

CHARLIE: Look, these guys have known hard times forever. Their parents went through it, maybe even before that too. They survive. Do it every time because they are workers. They will do whatever it takes, cut wood, clean floors, dig ditches. You name it they will do it.

In the face of so many hardships doing it for yourself is more likely to lead to a feeling of accomplishment and achievement. Relying on yourself is more important and reliable than relying on forces that you cannot control. Parents taught that hard work is rewarded by the personal satisfaction that comes directly from it. Indirectly, they teach a sense of selfhood that emerges from the way one works. What you do for a job is not as important as the way you work at it. Personal satisfaction, which is related to the FCWc system, is achieved by doing the best you can at any task. As seen in the interviews, few jobs or tasks would be considered demeaning. There are many stories of Acadian Americans taking on tasks at the workplace that are usually not required or expected of employees. The person will assume responsibility for these tasks because to work hard means to do a job as completely and as best as one can. Work is not bounded by job descriptions or an employer's expectations. It is an enactment of selfhood, family, culture, and morality. The stories about working were often about extending beyond what is expected at a job and working in a way that is consistent with the strong logical forces found in FCWc. Acadian Americans do not work differently in one place than they would at another. Work has the same forces at home, community, or at a job because working is what a person does in living a life. They live in a world that is without borders between family, culture, work, and church. There are strong logical forces that define the rules of action and communication for the Acadian Americans. The more traditional notions of work and family lack coherence for the Acadian Americans. It is within FCWc that they find the forces and rules that inform them how to live life as a good person would.

In this section the group members were talking about how their expectation for getting things done at home differed from other people's expectations. Here there is evidence of what should and should not be done within the home in relationship to one's family. Joan expresses rules that she uses that reflect structure and action for her in a particular episode of a mother and her family. These rules are called upon to guide her action, or in this case what action she would take.

THERESA: It bothers me. I feel bad for a little boy when he doesn't have an ironed shirt. I think his mother just takes the shirt out of the laundry basket and give it to him. I know they go to our school and they are not Acadian, they just don't know. Kids could make fun of him.

JOAN: But not all women are like that. I work with some they don't iron, they make TV dinners, but they are off at ceramics class, chairmen of clubs and committees. Drives me <u>NUTS</u>! You can only do extra things once your family is taken care of. You make sure you make a meal that is on the table make it the night before.

DORIS: You know what? You can drive yourself crazy about that. I feel guilty if we have left-overs two nights and not one night like I am not being the good wife. Not coming home and not making a good meal, you know.

JOAN: Not me, I feel like food is food, but when I see these women five nights a week and they worked all day and out of the five they go home two nights because the other nights they do this, this, and this. It's not they are doing this it's, . . it's just that (pause) I[

DORIS: [maybe that's their way of relaxing and we don't know how to do that.

JOAN: But <u>they need</u> to take care of their family, then do that. I can't handle them putting aside the supper, ironing and groceries. You want to do those things, go home and take care of what needs to be done first. I see this woman who is involved in every community thing there is but I look at her kid it annoys me. Fine but this kid never has a lunch, this kid has got a black bra on under her white blouse

ALL: (look at each other surprised, gasps are heard, then laughter)

JOAN: SEE! (stands-up and points at the others) Look what you're doing you are just like me! I want to say to her, instead of joining ten things and being in every community thing, take care of that kid and your family first!

ALL: (laughter)

DORIS: You are right I could never . . . no I could never allow that. <u>No!</u>

JOAN: I don't even know you that well, but I know I can drive to any of your houses right now and they would be neat, with everything done just so. I can tell this just by the way we are talking.

ALL: (All leaning forward toward Joan, nodding in agreement) some verbal cues of agreement.

Theresa: (Leans back in her chair) You are s::o right.

Stories here reveal that a good wife and mother is one who shops for groceries, prepares good meals, does not put aside preparing supper, or ironing in favor of doing things outside of the home. There is a strong sense of responsibility to work hard to raise your children, and to care for your family before you take care of your own needs and desires. More than just the responsibility, there are rules that are called upon when fulfilling a job of motherhood. For Joan and the others, mothers must supervise their children according to the rules within FCWc. This not only tells you how to enact an episode of parenting, but it also tells an Acadian American how to work at parenting, as well as things in and outside the home. It became clear to all of the members what Joan was speaking of when she related the story of the mother who had an active involvement outside of the home, and was not supervising her child as an Acadian-American mother would. When this event is viewed as situated within contexts of FCWc stories, Acadian-American ideas of parenting are revealed. The interactions throughout the transcript have a rhythm of exchange and turn taking that has each act serving as the antecedent for the next person to act, and each act directed toward an anticipated consequence. A CMM analysis of this section interprets the meanings informing the members' actions. In this section CMM reveals the rules Acadian Americans use to guide their interactions and achieve coherence. In Joan's rules there is a set of embedded contexts. The highest context is the family-cultural-work-church (FCWc) which organizations of relationships embody. These relationships develop in the action and there are either reconstituted or changed. Joan's understanding of the FCWc pattern may both have social and idiosyncratic features. Joan's autobiography is the next level of context that we see. The two lowest levels of context are the episode and a triad of acts. The triad of acts includes the antecedent act of condition, her own action, and an anticipated consequence or responding act. Initially the deontic operator for Joan is distinguished as obligatory as she talks about things a parent must choose to do. Joan's autobiography is near the same level as FCWc because Joan's point of view is constituted by her relationship to these areas. Selfhood for Acadian Americans is a representation of the FCWc. Clearly Joan is experiencing this action from a third person perspective when she speaking for all Acadian Americans. Her voice is not that of an individual *I* as it speaks the voice of the community. This is most evident when Joan speaks after Doris's comment about driving yourself crazy. She is not talking to Doris. She speaks for all Acadian Americans. Within this situated interaction these members speak to the group, and for the group. Joan's choice of action is to respond, "if you want to do those things [referring to relaxing or going out of the home in the evening] go home and take care of what needs to be done first." This has a strong prefigurative force as she is talking of the obligation that must occur before a person can act within this context. She is speaking of what tells her to act in this way for your family. The prefigurative force emanates from the sense of obligation she feels from definitions of self, and the relationship to FCWc. It is the sense that "I must do that." Joan may have anticipated what Doris's response, and all of the other participants' responses would be to the story of the mother who leaves home. This response reconstituted her familial-cultural understandings, and autobiography. Joan's verbal action and her nonverbal behavior form the context for the other participants' response. Her clarity of response, and the example of a non–Acadian-American mother elicited a response of agreement. Joan is speaking for FCWc and she speaks for all Acadian Americans. Joan seeks a consequence of confirmation from the members of what a mother must do.

Doris's comment in the beginning of the interaction is a direct response to Joan. Joan's comment serves at the antecedent for Doris's act to express how difficult it is to live according to the principles of Acadian American stories of mothers and parenting. Doris's rules are embedded in a context similar to Joan's. A statement like, you can drive yourself crazy, expresses the difficulties in living according to the principle that Joan states, of taking care of your family first. The deontic operator is legitimate as Doris is expressing a conflict that exists for most people. Doris speaks from a person position where she talks of the difficulties people share. Doris later agrees with this Acadian-American story, but she is seeking acknowledgment from others about the tension in living up to the story.

Joan speaks directly to the tension and difficulty Doris describes. It is likely that all of the members have felt this from time to time. However, her story of the mother who does not do all the things she is supposed to and then has a child in Catholic school wearing a black bra demonstrates the consequences of not following the rules within FCWc. This vivid story reaffirms the forces in the FCWc. This is not so much a representation of Joan's personal point of view as it represents a shared view among Acadian-American women and mothers. The act here is offered to reaffirm the importance of principles over the difficulties a person could experience. The gasp by all of the participants communicates a level of shock, which is a powerful expression of understanding and confirmation. This story and the communal reaction of shock resolves the conflict that Doris raises. However Joan's intended consequence of sharing a graphic story anticipated correctly that the members would confirm that living according to the principles is far better than giving in to the tension or conflict, driving yourself crazy.

This story had a reflexive effect on the participants, and there was a strong reflexive need for the continuation of Acadian-American practices of relationship to FCWc. The reflexive effects are most evident in the response to the story of the mother who does not take care of her child according to an Acadian-American story of parenting and work. The gasp by the participants also serves as a way to join in a clear and dynamic response that indicates a level of understanding and affirmation of the rules in FCWc. The rules determine for Joan and the others which specific behaviors ought to be enacted in present-day family situations. The others readily understood Joan's statement about the mother who goes out several nights a week. The meaning of this event was guided by rules that informed the participants that going out, and allowing a daughter to wear a black bra, are not what a mother does. What is seen here is a series of rules that together form a structure that guides the action in communication for the participants. Doris may have sought group support over the tension in living out the story, but she is able to act as part of the group and joins in after Joan relates the graphic story of what happens. We all see that the instrumental aspect of language is not capable of expressing what Doris is feeling; she is at a loss for words when she joins in with others and has a difficult time in stating what it would be like to be in the position of the mother who violated the principles.

The reflexive effects in this interaction allow the members to join in the episode Joan relates, and sustains Acadian-American stories of parenting and work. There is a conjoint creation of the story. The members here draw on grammatical abilities that they bring to this moment and they extend the comments of each other. They draw upon this grammatical ability to tell and extend the story, and they conjointly set for each other their notions of what a good person is. Their action together sustains and develops ideas of what a mother does and how she works in the FCWc set of rules.

During this part of the interview there was a high level of excitement among the members. They would share observations and continue the story another member had started. Reflexive needs are found in the importance the Acadian Americans share with regard to belonging to this community. Creating stories together, or continuing the stories, satisfies the need to be part of the community. The members are aware that the outside world may see parts of these stories and actions as nonsensical. How these Acadian-American stories are sustained when living in a world that is different from your own presents a challenge for these members. The members construct powerful ways of sustaining the stories inside their community. They are aware there are other ways to live a life, but there are stronger forces leading them to act in a manner to preserve the stories that are inherent in the FCWc. Sustaining and continuing these stories justifies the coherence of the patterns of behavior and actions that are part of Acadian-American life. The reflexive need is to belong and to continue these stories so as to make the world they live in a world that has logic even when threatened from outside. The people in the outside world will see Acadian-American stories of parenting and working as unnatural, and the members will laughingly say people see them as crazy. However the forces that are found within the FCWc are a powerful grammar that represents their story of living a life. Without a strong sense of belonging, these members and their culture are at risk. Many outside of the Acadian-American community see many of these actions as unnecessary or "crazy" ways of doing things. However the strength of the prefigurative forces tells many of the members that this is an effective way to live. As long as the members can sustain and continue the stories the logical force in FCWc is viable, as is their own selfhood. The reflexive need of belonging not only sustains individual stories, but it sustains the culture itself by extending its coherence for its members.

Communion

When looking at the interaction it is obvious that a change in the direction and flow of the communication occurs after Joan relates the story that caused the members to gasp. The shock expressed by the members serves as a punctuation point. From this point on there is a communal joining together. At the end of the last section of transcript Joan tells the others that she does not know them that well, but she can tell what their houses look like, meaning well-kept and in order. This is an important feature of this interaction. Prior to the interview most of these members only knew each other by name, but Joan can make this statement because she recognizes a shared bond among the participants. The bond is more than a shared heritage. These people share a story of what it is to live life as an Acadian American that has consistent rules and forces for action. The members also share a common understanding of the rules for action that are found within the expectations of FCWc. This became apparent to all the members through their interactions in the interview. They recognized the reflexive features in the interaction, and that they shared an understanding of Acadian-American stories of living a life. The members agree, and affirm Joan's observation about what their lives as Acadian Americans are like, and they recognize that they share stories for ways of acting. The intensity of the interaction is a critical feature of what is being conveyed. Joan physically stood up and addressed the others, and they gave her full attention by leaning forward in their chairs and listening intently to what she had to say. The other members regarded Joan's statement as legitimate. When Joan declared that they were all alike, the members connected to her statement, and to each other through shifts in their body posture, nodding, sounds of agreement, and other nonverbal actions. These are meaningful aspects of their communication that should be accounted for in making sense of this interaction. Theresa's final statement was delivered slowly and as a thoughtful reflection, stating Joan was "s::o right." This response appeared to indicate a deep level of appreciation for what Joan had said. Theresa's emphatic response to Joan's comment, and the actions of the others, reaffirms what was being said and an understanding of what they share.

As a participant-observer of this interaction, and at a few other moments in the interviews, I recognized a level of connection among the members that had a depth unlike other aspects of their conversation. This deeply felt way of talking occurred when they would discuss ways that they were alike, and common stories they shared. The interactions at these points would center on stories about moral choices, and how the choices would be resolved in a manner consistent with what they were taught and believed. Members would extend the story and thus affirm the speaker's comments. This action served a reflexive need to reaffirm their beliefs as well. It was in the depth of this grammar that notions of working, living, family, and culture come to be more fully expressed among the members.

Throughout all of the interviews there were episodes like the one identified above where it may be said the members share a communion, much like the sacrament found in their Catholic faith. The Catholic Church regards the sacrament of the Holy Eucharist, or Holy Communion, as essential to living a good life. The sacrament is regarded as the sign and sharing of divine life, and the unity of people with God. It is through this sacrament that the church is thought to live and grow. Holy Communion is believed to be morally necessary for salvation as it aids the person in resisting temptation and avoiding grievous sin (Remy, 1910). More than just an individual experience, the sacrament provides members of the Church with the opportunity to gather together and form one "holy, catholic and apostolic church." Holy Eucharist serves as means to help the faithful recognize the place they have in the community and celebrate their community bond. Teaching the power and the beliefs surrounding this sacrament requires that the Church use the process of catecheses to instill faith in the community members so they may realize this commemoration as the true center of Christian life (Broderick, 1987). It can be said that the spiritual life of the faithful is confirmed through the sacrament of Communion.

The members share this communion by talking of ways they are alike, and what they share in terms of strong moral forces that lead them to act in ways that are Acadian-American. They share stories of how life must be lived and is so doing they reaffirm their ways of feeling, talking, and acting. To be Acadian-American is to live by the forces found in FCWc. Religious beliefs, and in this case religious sacraments, are active and inseparable aspects of their lives. The sharing that is done in the interviews has a reflexive effect to sustain ideas and stories of what it is to live a good life. The members called upon their grammatical abilities and common understandings to conjointly act in ways that a hard-working person acts. The reflexive needs are evident in the conversants' strong desire to belong to this community and sustain Acadian-American stories of living in a way that affirms the coherence of patterns of working, family life, culture, and religious belief. Sharing a communion of ideas, and reaffirmations of what they believe, satisfies this reflexive need. Corresponding to Catholic Liturgy there is a "preaching of the word" that accompanies the sacrament and ritual of Mass. What the members talk about here is like a preaching of the word found in the religious ritual. Joan speaks for all Acadian Americans and reaffirms the forces and ways of acting that a mother must do. The others recognize this and agree with her in this communion. These exchanges, much like Holy Communion, are more than individual experiences. These are moments when the members come together and recognize the depth of their community.

The catechesis of this communion transpires within the institutions of family, culture, school and church. The interaction and stories that have been shared within these institutions have lead to strong prefigurative forces that tell the members how to act. Sharing a communion in their interaction reaffirms their actions and helps them live a life that is morally coherent with the force of FCWc.

Within Catholic observance, the Holy Eucharist is the source of all other sacraments and an inseparable bond exists between this sacrament and all others that are practiced by members of the Catholic faith (Broderick, 1987). This inseparable feature of Holy Eucharist is like the relationship among FCWc. The communion the members share in this episode links the religious beliefs with all other aspects of FCWc. This communion with its reflexive features serves to extend the members' ways of acting in a coherent and meaningful way.

This part of the transcript demonstrates the ability of interaction to reconstitute the self within the rules of the social group. In this interaction, Acadian American ways of living are reaffirmed. What is worth noting here is that the members described these duties as obligations much like the ones their parents felt. There is a link to the past, but life is not static for the Acadian Americans. These are people who are actively involved in a joint process of adapting Acadian-American stories to new challenges. They must keep a story alive that is coherent with the forces in FCWc, but they must do so in a way that makes sense in the world in which they live and not the past. Much like their parents, the duties of parenting are entwined with the action of working, both at home and at a place of employment, to provide for family and to sustain Acadian-American stories of living. Parents must work outside the home to provide the things family members need, and a parent must work at home to sustain the FCWc stories. The role of parents will be expanded in this chapter to include the things that can and must be done to raise children, and illustrate the important bond between families and the Acadian-American community. The primacy of parenting-working sustains the FCWc stories, and allows the culture to withstand threats to ways of doing things. The grammatical abilities the members share sustain their individuality and the community's stories of how episodes of action must go. A story such as this one reinforces coherent ways of acting that arise in the interaction process among the members. Here this situated encounter both constitutes and reaffirms the actions of parenting-working.

The Laughing Game

In this section of transcript a theme emerges in many of the accounts which will be referred to as the laughing game. The form of the game is that a person laughs at how intensely they work. They declare it eccentric then laugh, but go on to affirm it as the right way to act. Within these episodes, another Acadian American may see it as "crazy," or describe it as "nuts", but they go on to affirm it as well. The laughing and affirmation are the reflexive effect that comes back to speakers when they act in certain ways. In the last transcript provided above, Doris states that you can drive yourself crazy, but acknowledges, "I feel guilty and I am not being the good wife." There are practices an Acadian American must engage in to live as a good person; many of these practices may seem eccentric when compared to how others outside of their culture act. By living among members of other cultures they come to recognize just how their practices differ. The laughing game is played to acknowledge these differences, and also serves a function within the Acadian-American community to embrace and affirm their actions as peculiar to them.

The laughing game follows a sequence when it is enacted among the Acadian Americans. In the *opening act* there is a statement made about an episode and an individual's personal feeling about the episode that is tied to the logical forces in FCWc. It is common for another speaker to counter the first speaker's observation, and then a comment is extended by either the first speaker or the person who countered the original statement. The *acknowledgment act* is signaled by the laugh itself, which all parties engage in. This laugh acts as a statement of reaffirmation. The *closure act* signals the end of the game and the subject is no longer discussed. Sometimes the members signaled closure by making a general statement about life, or a question such as "what can you do?" There are times in the interaction that the laugh itself serves as an abrupt ending to the game.

This game can also be played in other ways and with slight variations. At one point with this group, Theresa told the members that she and her husband had talked things over, and they were going to start relaxing more beginning next month. As soon as Theresa had made the statement, the other group members broke out in loud laughter, and Theresa joined in the laughing. The others, kidding her, stated that she could never do it. Theresa then acknowledged that she works too hard, but affirmed that at least she can think about relaxing. The acts here are elements of the episode, which is the action of affirming working hard as the right thing. The antecedent is declaring working hard as crazy or eccentric. The laughing game becomes a fixed pattern which is legitimate to the Acadian Americans. The affirmation by others is a consequence that sustains the game and has a reflexive effect on all of the members in the game.

The game is played many times in the interviews and always serves as affirmation that working hard is the right thing to do no matter how odd it seems to others.

Men, Women, Families, and Work

Males that were interviewed also expressed a strong obligation to the family, and a strong moral force as their fathers had. However the males placed more emphasis on work outside of the home, much as their fathers had. There were stories of these men working multiple jobs as their fathers had to provide for their families. When asked how work at home differs from working at their job, the responses generally described working around the house as something that must be done because it's part of the responsibility of ownership. Although they made a distinction between workplace and home, the intensity at which they work and how they work remains the same for them in both places. All cultures have tensions within their practices, and this appears to be a tension within the culture for Acadian-American males. The story is told of not doing much at home—yet there are accounts of working hard around the house and working at the same levels at home or at work. The men also called on the laughing game when they talked about working at home. They would first state they did not work as intensely at home as they did at their jobs, but then they would relate stories of hard work around the house. They would say how crazy it was that they did not know how to relax. Others would join in then reaffirm the level of working. The laughing game in this instance is used to address the tension between work in different places and affirm that men work hard at home as well.

When asked if there were differences in the ways Acadian-American men and women work at home, males and females alike responded they all work hard, but that there are differences in roles. The differences generally follow patterns of traditional American families, where mothers perform the majority of the housekeeping tasks, and fathers take care of yard work and household and automobile maintenance. Some variations and changes in the gender roles are emerging within this present generation. More females are working outside the home, as is seen in the wider American culture. This may be a signal of change in the FCWc pattern for Acadian Americans.

The Bond between Families and Community

Parents were described as stern and as disciplinarians, yet there were many stories of families extending generosity and concern to other Acadian families within a neighborhood. These acts of generosity are guided by moral forces of obligation that lead to action, and rules that guide the action. However it was revealed in all of the interviews that Acadian Americans have a strong sense of independence and pride which shapes the rules for how an act of generosity is to take place. The issue came up when members described their family working through tough times, and never going to anyone for help, especially public welfare or social service agencies, because of their pride. Seeking help could be viewed as an admission that you didn't work hard enough, and were unable to provide for your family. As this issue was explored, it emerged that you did not ask an Acadian neighbor for help, but all families would "watch out" for each other. When asked how this might play out, members stated you would notice kids wearing the same clothes day after day, and you'd know that their parents were not able to afford new clothes like a coat or mittens that fit. In this case, your mother would knit a pair of mittens, or find a coat that was not being used and give it directly to the child when they were playing outside. It was seldom given to or through the parents. The members described another scenario, when families might not have enough to eat. Neighbors would notice if a family did not have much food. In your building, you could smell what was being made for meals, or you would notice that groceries seldom came into the house. When this happened it was common to prepare extra food and bring it to these families in need. It would be said that this is extra, or I made a mistake and made too much of this, and it will go to waste if you don't take it. People were careful not to offer food or clothing as handouts. There was an obligation to offer help, but rules governed the interaction so that the donor would allow the recipient to maintain their independence and pride. There are prefigurative forces that direct Acadian Americans to respond in a specific way to other members of their culture when things are not going well. The family extends itself beyond confines usually found in other cultures because of its inseparable nature with its culture. The logical forces are extended, and members act in prescribed ways.

There were numerous stories among the participants of someone in their immediate family or extended families taking in non-related Acadian children and raising them. This usually occurred when mothers died, or were gravely ill. Families care for children of these other families for extended periods of time, or until the child reached adulthood. This was usually done if the children did not have any relatives in the United States. Children would join another family because their father worked more than one job that prevented them from providing a home at standards common to Acadian households. These fathers of motherless children would provide financial support, but the new family would assume all other responsibilities.

THERESA: In my family I have an uncle who is not really my uncle. His mother died when he was young. My grandmother, who was his neighbor, took him in because his father could not care for him. They weren't related. I think they came from the same town in New Brunswick, but there was no relation. My grandmother knew she had to help out this little boy and she did. There was no legal adoption or anything. His father even moved to Maine for another job and he stayed here with my grandmother. She raised him like it was her son. His father would send a little money and see him, but he lived with[

DORIS: [My husband's family did the same thing. There was a little girl whose mother was in and out of the state hospital for something. So my mother in-law raised her, gave her a home, and even paid for her wedding I think. Very generous, very. They just loved the idea of family and would never turn the kids over to the state. They took care of each other.

LINDA: This was more common than you would think. There were many families that did this.

The members interpreted this action as evidence of the importance of family to their parents and the strength of the community. Members saw this practice as evidence of how highly valued families were to Acadians. While there is little doubt that the concept of family is important, the actions on the part of the Acadian families show how the concept of family is not bounded and care is offered to all members of the culture.

Signs of Success

The participants in the interviews described Acadian Americans as frugal, and not ostentatious in terms of the clothes they wear, cars they drive, or the homes they live in. Recognizing that these objects may signify success for most Americans, participants were asked if there were better signs of success. The responses in all of the groups were that family closeness is the greatest sign of success. One participant stated proudly that the front of her mother's house looks like a used car lot every Sunday morning after church because the entire family comes to visit. Many of the participants talked about similar family gatherings occurring on a frequent basis. Members in all of the groups described this as the greatest sign of success for a family, and stated that this is much different from and better than what other people would see as success.

Another participant stated, with sadness, that her family is not as close as she would like them to be. She talks with her mother almost daily by telephone and regularly visits her, and has weekly contact with her siblings. For this Acadian American there is not enough contact in those relationship to satisfy her reflexive need. There would have to be certain responses present for her to feel her reflexive needs are being met. These unsatisfied reflexive needs means she does not get to develop the story in a direction that she wants the story to go.

In adult life there is a strong prefigurative force to work hard and support your family. The reflexive needs continue throughout your life and are seen in a measure of success which is the closeness among family members. The reflexive need is to continue the relationship and the reflexive effects are apparent in the relationship among family members. This strong obligation to family continues throughout the course of a life.

MARIE: Some people just don't understand how close we (Acadian Americans) are to our families. Christ, my sisters and I call Mom every day. Seems as people leave home they drift away from their family; not us.

JOSEPH: I visit my parents four, five times a week. We are close. Seems most of us are (referring to Acadian Americans). Family is important through your whole life. You don't just get raised and say see you later. It gets closer all the time and it is something you are proud of.

As described by Pearce (1989) families are a primary locus of institutionalized coherence. The parents' perspective on the world and their practices when acting into that world have a lasting impact on children if that view has a high degree of coherence with others. The family, and the adults' role defined in relation to the family, served as the centerpiece for creating identity, transmitting cultural resources, practices, and moral orders. Coherence is present throughout the family, but what makes the experience of the Acadian Americans somewhat different from most other cultural groups is that the coherence extends throughout the culture itself. The impact of this dynamic has influenced the shared grammar of what work means. How to work hard was taught through interaction with family, culture, and church, and it is sustained as a necessity for family, individual and the community. Work has prominence in the Acadian-American family and culture, and this prominence is transmitted to children in the form of an institutionalized coherence. These stories of hardworking mothers and fathers demonstrate the moral orders that were present in family life. The deontic operators present here were conscious and could be viewed as obligatory. The force that served as an impetus for women to wash clothes on a scrub board until their hands blistered, or for men to work multiple jobs, was a sense of obligation to your family, and the importance of doing the best you could do. The FCWc stories inform families how to act, and what needs to be done to live within as a member of this community. The similarity among the stories illustrated how similar rules and forces were used by the many families represented in the interviews.

Chapter 6

Stories of Church and Work

THE STORIES TOLD IN THE INTERVIEWS showed that church is not independent of family, culture, or working. It has a strong relation to these domains as an institution that expresses, teaches, and reinforces shared beliefs among the members of the community. The Acadian Americans are members of the Roman Catholic Church, and they established strong church communities in the cities and towns they moved to. As stated above, the church became and remains for many a central point of their life. Within this city, as in other New England cities that the Acadians emigrated to, many lived in housing that physically surrounded the church, or within walking distance. In these cities and towns the church served as the center of religious life, social life, and the community itself.

The Catholic Church is not a monolith, and Catholicism when practiced can take on different forms and practices among the members of its community. In this case, the Acadians supported their own church, while in this small city there were other churches that served the needs of other immigrant groups such as the Polish and Irish. The Acadians had and continue with an inseparable bond between their family, culture, ideas of working, and their Catholicism. Acadian practices differ from the practices of other Catholics.[1] This may be attributed to their history and the intertwined relationship among FCWc. Catholicism serves a different function for Acadians than it does for many other Catholics. In this city a parochial school has served children consistently since 1903, and remains a vibrant part of the parish, serving an important function in extending Acadian stories. Participants in the interviews spoke of a strong affiliation with the church and school, and that there is an enduring link between them and what these institutions provide and represent. As indicated above, members saw home, church, and school as an extension of each other, and a consistent message was reinforced in each of these settings.

There were many stories about the church and its priests and the nuns who worked in both the church and the school. The priests and the nuns taught what the expectations were for both children and adults. These religious figures played a central role in imparting the practical forces of FCWc. The members did not see a distinction between schoolwork, work at home, or work at a job. Work is regarded as whatever must be done, and done with full attention.

Interview participants shared stories of how particular priests and nuns influenced their lives, always talking much more about this particular church, school, and its clergy, as opposed to the larger concepts of Catholicism. Members spoke fondly of "old-fashioned" priests who cared about the parish. The members attributed this to a different time. Below is a section from the transcript describing an old-fashioned priest, the relationship people had to them, and comparing them to the new kind of priest.

JOSEPH: Things were different back when we were kids because we had priests like Father A. and Father G. They were big parts of our life. Seemed they were at everything you did.

CHARLIE: The old guys really seemed to care and get involved with every little thing about our lives, the school . . . the church fair. Even our parents seemed to fear them when they spoke.

JOSEPH: I think they respected them more than were afraid of them. Those guys really were priests. Speak French to the old timers, loved the Mass, the kids, and the school. Kept us in line. Nowadays it runs like a business. Things have to make profits, golf fund-raisers. Christ, what the hell did our fathers know about golf, they worked like animals. Golf, Jesus!

MARIE: Hey that's why lately I go to Mass don't get involved with these new guys. They do have a different way of thinkin' what this church is about. . . . I guess they have to act like business people, but maybe we would respect them more. They are just not the role model the other priests were. I don't even think all of these new guys are Acadian.

The grammar of an old-fashioned priest describes a priest who is perceived as being concerned with the people in the neighborhood, is pious, doesn't talk about money, and loves what he is doing. Members indicated that a recent decision to end masses that were conducted in French was terrible, and typical of the kind of changes they have witnessed. This was described as a loss to the older parishioners. The tension regarding the newer type of priest can be attributed to the desire to fulfill the reflexive needs of sustaining an Acadian American story of Catholicism. The newer priests may be concerned with larger issues that are faced by the Catholic Church in general, or sustaining a Church that now serves a diverse population. Even with their grumbling, the members continue to respect the newer priests and there is little doubt that the Church remains an important aspect of the lives of these individuals.

Foundational Beliefs and Working

Several questions were asked in the interviews about faith and its influence on ideas of work and work ethic. In this section of the transcript members are talking about how their religious beliefs affected the way in which they work.

JOAN: You are brought up to believe that it is very important to God to take care of your family. That is number one to Him, children, and taking care of each other, being there for each other.

DORIS: Haven't we all chosen community-oriented jobs? All helping jobs[

LINDA: [and I am not surprised we are doing what we are doing[

JOAN: [and hard work is part of that, of who you are. Not doing that, you are breaking one of the biggest laws in our faith—to help others.

LINDA: It goes back to what they teach you when you are in school—being honest, helping out. It's like Girl Scouts, which I think is a great organization. It encompasses all that I teach my daughter: to be honest, be a friend, helping people that need help.

INTERVIEWER: *Could you do that being a stockbroker, or salesperson?*

JOAN: No, that's why we can't be one

LINDA: You wouldn't last I mean[

THERESA: [maybe a real estate agent. I would find you the best house that's a good job[

JOAN: [but what if you had to lie? I couldn't do it[

THERESA: [I would have to be honest[

LINDA:]but then you might not sell a lot of houses[

JOAN: [I would starve. I would only sell one a year. I couldn't do a lot of jobs.

THERESA: Catholicism has had a foundation in our lives[

DORIS: [I think so.

JOAN: I would say that is 99 percent of the reason we work like we do, think like we do, it intertwines with the lying, see I could never be a lawyer because I could never lie. But I could do it if they let me protect the good ones.

THERESA: There were years I did not go to church but I came back and it was better than ever.

JOAN: For us it wasn't just school. It was home and for some it was just school

INTERVIEWER: *What made coming back to church better than ever?*

Theresa: I don't know . . . It all made sense now. Especially when I had kids, a house, a job. What was being said in church helped me to be better at these things.

INTERVIEWER: *Is Catholicism the same in all churches?*

DORIS: No, I go to a new church now, well, for the past fifteen years since we moved. I like the church I am a part of, but it teaches different things in some ways. There aren't as many Acadians there to begin with so it's not a church that serves one culture. It's Catholic doctrine, but it doesn't have the feel our church had.

INTERVIEWER: *In what ways does it feel different from the church you were raised in?*

DORIS: I don't know, to begin with the church fair doesn't have the Acadian food (laughs). There isn't a school so maybe that's part of it too. It seems a little more liberal. We had deacons and small changes like that before the other church did. I like it and I go mostly because it was the church my husband went to when he was a little boy and through his whole life. I don't know, it's just different.

There are several points in this section of transcript that highlight the close relationship of religious belief to work, family, and culture. In Joan's opening statement it is apparent that religious beliefs are closely related to other stories the participants told of family life. There is a link between taking care of a family, raising children, and others as seen in the stories of families extending help to other Acadian families in need. What is also apparent is that the members see their job choice as impacted by religious beliefs. This also came up in a nonprofessional group. A member of the nonprofessional group, who works assembling fire alarms, stated that she works hard because that fire alarm may save someone's life. Joan again makes comments that show this link between hard work makes you who you are and it is part of your faith. Joan speaks for all Acadian Americans by talking of the rule or in this case the "laws" that guide their faith. These laws serve as a strong deontic operator of obligation.

The professional participants credit this family-culture-religious belief as reason for the jobs they chose as helping professionals. However, the nonprofessionals do much the same and adopt the perspective that you can help others in all kinds of jobs as long as the job allows you to be honest. The members regarded many jobs as compromising your ability to act honestly. In this section there is discussion among the members about jobs they could never do, such as stockbroker, salesperson, or lawyer. There is a belief that those occupations require that at times you must be deceitful which violates the rules of faith, family, and community. Later in the interviews there was more evidence of lack of trust of certain occupations when the Acadian Americans discuss how difficult it is for them to buy products or services from others outside of their community. This concern with honesty has influenced these individuals to choose, or perhaps avoid, certain occupations. There is evidence of reflexive effects when Theresa is asked if she could lie if she was a real estate agent. She responds that she would have to be honest and feels she would not sell many houses. The rules of Acadian-American life continue to guide job choices, action, and the interaction. Making money, or a job title, does not make you worthwhile. The rewards you receive from helping others are not in the amount of money you earn, but in fulfilling obligations to community, family, and religion. This is what makes you a good person and satisfies a sense of selfhood.

Theresa makes the comment that Catholicism is the foundation for their work, and Joan follows by saying that it's 99 percent of the reason they work as they do. There is a strong force in their lives that is embedded in FCWc. When asked if all churches are the same, they see differences. The Catholicism they are familiar with appears to be the foundation for what they believe and how they act at work, within their family, and their culture. Catholicism in this church and community has differences from other Catholic churches for Acadian Americans. The actions of the members of this church represent a different version of rules for action from what may be found in other Catholic churches. These rules inform members how they should live their faith, enact episodes of family life, work, and community life. An Acadian story of what Catholicism is is seen in the conversations describing an old-fashioned priest who has different values and acts in ways that differ from those of the newer priests, or things the members can and cannot do because of their faith and beliefs.

In the structure of the Catholic Church, priests are assigned to a parish by a bishop and the congregation has little input in the process. Members of the Acadian-American community can point to a priest and say that is not how a priest should act; in so doing they make judgments about what is Catholicism and how it should be lived. Their version of Catholicism follows the structure that guides the Acadian-American community and the inseparable nature of FCWc.

Theresa made a comment above that what was being said in church made sense now, and especially in light of her responsibilities of raising children, maintaining a house, and working at her job. She also went on to say that church helped her to do these things better. This statement demonstrates how religion reinforces the logical forces found in FCWc, and the inseparable nature of these aspects of living a life for Acadian Americans. Church has a reflexive effect on her stories of how to fulfill these obligations in a way that a good person would.

The Nexus of Church, Belief, and Community

The participants relayed stories of a former pastor who sternly guided his parish and enacted rules that reaffirmed their notions of selfhood. Members talked about a large migration from New Brunswick that took place in the middle 1960s. The families that came to the area were described as very poor. The members spoke of one family whose children had very little clothing. Their mother kept their clothes clean and ironed, but the clothes were old, worn, and didn't match. The pastor, who also served as the principal of the school, decided to require that all children in the school wear uniforms. The members saw his policy as a direct result of the ridicule the children faced because their clothing was different. This action indicates the strength of the moral forces in Acadian Americans' lives. The consequence of the pastor's action was that all children in the school would look the same. The likelihood of teasing was minimized and the pastor imposed prefigurative force on the community. These prefigurative forces guided actions and strengthened a communal bond and the rules that told members they must be accepting of others in their community.

Members of another group recounted how their church and religion made their lives different from other teens in the city.

JOSEPH: Being one of the French kids from Holy Rosary made life a lot different. You didn't get away with the things the other kids could. Hey, you were there (directing the comment to Charlie). Remember the night, we were out of high school, and we were hanging around downtown with a bunch of kids sitting in cars in the bank parking lot. Father A goes to the bank to make a night deposit. He sees us in Pauly's father's car, taps on the window and says "you guys come with me." We followed him back to the church and he made us work setting up for the church fair or something.

CHARLIE: Oh God yes I remember that. We thought we were in trouble. He never said a word other than, it's a waste of time to hang around down there, and you have better things to do. He put us to work and we stayed out of trouble.

JOSEPH: We respected him. Tell you the truth feared him. The other kids gave us a hard time in school on Monday. Goddamn priest on a Saturday night makes us go back to the church and work while the other kids are raising hell, and we did it. Imagine that.

The members spoke of this priest as most people would talk about a stern parent. At the time of this episode these boys had graduated from the parochial school and were attending the local public high school. As the pastor and leader of this church he is regarded as an important figure in their community, family, and lives. In this episode the pastor serves as much of a disciplinarian as parents were within a family. These members respected and followed the direction of their church leader. He was described as working hard at serving his community, and as doing a lot for the people of the parish. The way he worked hard to fulfill his obligations was seen as worthy of their respect. The members talked of other priests who they saw working for different reasons, such as raising money, their own promotion within the dioceses, or reasons that were not consistent with their views of how a person works in the world. It can be said that this former pastor lived a story of what a priest should do in light of an Acadian-American story.

The Catechism of Working

The Acadian Americans in these interviews spoke of the importance of the school in their life. Here is a section of the transcript from a group when the members were asked about the relationship between work and their religious faith. This group is made up of professional men in their thirties who attended college, but returned to live and work in this community. One of the members is part owner of a family business, and the other is an engineer. This group is referred to as Group 3. They begin to talk about the importance of their school in making them who they are:

PAUL: The nuns in the school instilled morals in us, and I owe a lot to the school. I see a difference between being Catholic and a member of Holy Rosary. I wouldn't have been sent there if I wasn't Catholic, but the morals instilled in us were very important to how we live our lives today.

RENE: We were taught respect. We respected people, what people did for us, property and that if you work hard good things come to you.

PAUL: My children will go to that school because I owe a lot to it, and my sisters have said the same thing. It was the little things that helped me. We had school uniforms and I think the way a kid dresses influences the way he behaves and the fact that our parents had to spend money for us to get an education meant a lot to us.

RENE: Many of the kids' parents had to work extra to send the kids there, or had to work at bingo and the fair to get credits toward the tuition.

INTERVIEWER: *What makes you owe a lot? Your parents paid the tuition, you followed the rules, yet you feel you owe?*

PAUL: I am still involved; I participate in the fairs. When I say that I owe a lot, I think the things I have today I wouldn't have had if I had not gone through there. I would have been brought up with different ideas and mores. I wouldn't have had self-discipline and the interaction with people, if it wasn't for those things instilled in my mind at a very young age. I wouldn't have been as successful as I have been.

RENE: I don't feel I owe in the same regard as he does, but I noticed differences in behavior between public school and parochial school children. You don't get away with anything there and it carried over to home. I didn't get away with anything there either. The transition to High School (public) was weird. You carried on with the respect, and we didn't take advantage of the freedom there. You could pick out the kids from Catholic school and public school kids.

INTERVIEWER: *What told you there was a difference?*

PAUL: The way they held themselves, more self respect, respected authority [

RENE: [I noticed the kids who worked harder on homework were from the Catholic school.

PAUL: We were quickly accepted though because you didn't make trouble. You got along with everyone.

Rene: Remember when they would have the city-wide Olympics for school kids. The public school kids would be running all over the place, and we would sit in the bleachers waiting quietly for our events.

The members talked of morals being instilled in them while in school. Teachers relied on the practical forces in order to have children enact an Acadian story. The rules for all domains of FCWc are consistent, and working hard is an expected action within all of these settings. The school is an extension of the church, or even of the religion itself. The building that houses the school is next door to the church, and the school activities are centered on the religious beliefs, holidays, and events in the church. Rene's comment that what goes on in the school is carried on in the home is a testament to the unified relationship between religion, family, culture and work.

Here the members are seeing the school's role as teaching respect for people and property, and that good things happen when you work hard. These are many of the things that the family teaches its children. Members, speaking as parents in the interviews, stated that they point out to their children all the things they have as a result of hard work, and the importance of doing things for yourself. The sign of success for this school may be similar to the signs of success for families. Here we see members who state they owe a lot to the school, some are present by volunteering, and many say they will send or have sent their children there. Just as families measure their success by children that return to visit regularly, the school and the church have the same stories of people returning, which is much like the signs of success for Acadian-American families.

The school fulfilled a critical role in the teaching of morals. Sets of rules that are taught in the home, church, and culture are made much more explicit to the children through classroom instruction, and a process of inculcation. There are parts of the interviews where members describe these morals as a "ball and chain" because of how they are present in all you do, and sometimes prevented you from doing what you wanted. Within this transcript Rene recalls the city-wide Olympics, and at these events he recalled children from other schools running around while the children from this Acadian Catholic School were sitting quietly waiting to participate. Rene felt the children knew the rules for behavior and acted accordingly. The logical forces the children called upon blocked certain types of actions. One member talked of a memory of being a child and seeing candy bars in a store. She wanted to steal the candy as she had seen other, non-Acadian children do. However, she stated she couldn't bring herself to do it, and kept saying to herself one day she would do it. This member talked of a force that stopped her, which she described as her parents' voice or that of the church pastor. The deontic operators for children appear to come from beyond their control. In these cases there is a moral force that was taught to them through FCWc. This force blocked them from acting in a way they may want to, or other children would. This prefigurative force tells them how they should act. The school played a critical role in teaching children what is expected of them and how they should act in all places. However, the school shares another critical role with the family and culture, and that is working hard at school tasks, in your home, and at your job, is how a person must act in the world. This ability to work hard remains the same in all places you live.

Morals are initially described as something that was instilled, and later they take on an outward sign when Paul makes the statement about uniforms. Paul credits the uniform as an influence on the way children behave. Although he did not discuss this statement in great depth, uniforms indicate belonging to this school, and participating in its rules and expectations for behavior. As there are differences in the ways children act, there are clear signs, like a uniform, which distinguishes a group of people from others. It is noteworthy that Paul regards uniforms as influencing behavior, and the similarity of this theme with the story of the pastor who required all children in the school to wear uniforms to minimize differences among them.

The members maintained that they saw differences between them and other students when they went on to high school, or met other children who were not part of the Acadian-American community. The differences may be attributed to the logical forces and moral orders that guided their behavior. The members did not report having any difficulties in high school with either adults or other students. They felt they had developed an ability to get along with others. The report about life in high school had similarities to the life their parents live with non-Acadians. Their parents learned that if you work hard, never complain, do extra if it is needed, respect people in authority, and do not challenge others you will get along with others. Their action in high school was much the same as their parents' actions at work. These features have given Acadian Americans a high degree of success in managing interpersonal relationships with others. Later in this chapter, there is evidence that Acadian Americans experience certain tensions and frustrations with others outside of their community. Enacting an Acadian-American story of working hard ensures coherence within their family and community, but when interacting with others outside of your community a degree of conciliation is required; you are not allowed to express these frustrations directly to that person. Members described a conciliatory relationship with people outside of their community. There are stories of interaction guided by not challenging others, saying yes even when you believe they may be wrong, and being as agreeable to people as you can be. As highlighted in chapter 1, Acadians have a history of not challenging other groups for jobs, and to be Acadian has been said is to go unnoticed. Their focus on their family and community is most important to them, and they have adopted the practices of not complaining and making the best of what life has given. Many times in the interviews there appears a hesitancy to be involved with issues outside of their community. The members state they generally avoid management positions, politics, and trade with non-Acadians. However, there is no evidence of animosity or lack of willingness to cooperate with others outside of their community. This may be attributed to their long history of isolation, and hardship, which led to stories of doing things for yourself. Given the historical features, and the practice of not complaining, there are indications of different types of relationships being formed outside of the community.

The direction and role of their elementary school has recently changed. The school continues in its fused relationship with the church, but also accepts children from surrounding towns and various religious denominations. Some of the members have expressed concerns that the original purpose has changed, but there is agreement that the school still continues to provide an emphasis on discipline and hard work. It is still seen as having a capacity to instill morals, but these morals have been extended beyond those of the Acadian American community. Members talked of how the school is becoming a place for upper-class families to send their children. People outside of the Acadian-American community selecting the school for their children is received with mixed feelings by the members. They saw this as an affirmation that morals and hard work are valued in the world, and people recognize that Acadian-Americans know about this. However, there was talk about tuition increases that may make it difficult for Acadian-American children to attend the school. Concern was expressed that the school may be losing its focus as a part of the Acadian-American community.

There is little doubt that the elementary school played a major role in the catechesis of morals and logical forces found in the FCWc. The school was important in teaching children the rules of how working hard contributed to living a life.

Chapter 7

Stories of Motivated People

In the interviews the way that Acadian Americans work was explored, and whether these ways of working differ from how other people work. The answer came back that Acadians point with pride to a strong work ethic. This strong work ethic has its own grammar. The groups described the strong work ethic as working long days at a job and at home, and all things must be done to the best of your ability. Stories were shared about not being able to go on vacation unless the house was cleaned thoroughly and all the laundry was done. Other members said you work at something as long as it takes to complete a job, no matter how long it takes. When directly asked how Acadian Americans work differently from other people, the following account was given:

DORIS: A lot of them know how to take charge[

THERESA: [They are motivated

DORIS: [Somebody will volunteer to be the chair of the committee[

JOAN: [They do the extra piece and not complain, they give the extra[

DORIS: [They are not the person who sits back and listens to what everyone else has to say, they pitch in[

JOAN: [They never complain about doing things. They always find a way.

INTERVIEWER: *Do others think of this kind of person as bossy?*

LINDA: Most of the times they are the organizers, they are motivated and get people excited and get people to join and you see them as team workers. They are not telling people or telling them directly, they know how to include the group and they don't direct anybody. They don't tell people what to do, but they say here is a plan and if we work together . . . or how can we split up the work, and they do it in a friendly kind of way.

JOAN: You ask if people can do something and if they don't follow through you do it.

The response by the group described a way of acting that they termed "motivated." This term came up in all of the groups, which indicates it is widely used and understood. In an interaction where a motivated person is present there appears to be a great deal of coordination as the motivated person has to include others—not direct them, but assume responsibility for what happens or doesn't happen. Another group offered the comment that if people do not follow through you must finish the task. A motivated person assumes responsibility for finishing what the group set out to accomplish. The members expressed a concern about not appearing to be "bossy." Motivated people must be direct in an episode of acting as a motivated person, but they do not want to upset others. Others may become upset by someone who acts superior, or if they act as if they have all the answers. It is important in this episode to show emotions of genuine concern for others, and for what is best for the group or the community. The forces for a motivated person are prefigurative forces. The person knows they must act this way because it is the most effective way to act, and it is respectful of others in the setting. The moral order here informs the individual of what they must do and must not do when interacting with a group to get a job done. Other Acadian Americans usually understand the rules of action, but non-Acadians often do not understand them in the same way. The implications for Acadian Americans are discussed later in this section.

A motivated person has a sense of what needs to be done without being told by others, and works diligently no matter what the job is. Here is one group relating an example of that motivated worker:

JOSEPH: You all know C.D., the guy who worked at the hockey rink. He lost his job at Digital when they laid off all those people . . . a high paying one, and the only job he could find was at the state skating rink, keeping it clean, making ice, you know, kind of a maintenance position. It was a position that you would think was beneath him. He was probably making a fraction of what he was making at Digital. Then get this. He goes to the hockey rink and cleans all the scuff-marks the pucks made off the boards[

MARIE: [Yeah my husband always talked about this.

JOSEPH: It didn't matter that this job was beneath what we wanted to do. Then Digital calls him back for a few months. The rink looks like shit again. One night I am there to pick up my kids and the place looks good again. Here comes C out of the office. He just looks at me and says I am back another lay-off[

CLAIRE: [My husband came home one night and said, C.D. is back at the rink, and I asked how is he. My husband said I don't know I didn't see him, but I know he is back because the locker room smells like that orange disinfectant and the boards were scrubbed down again. Sure enough, I ran into his sister the next day and she tells me he is back (laughs)

ALL: (Laugh)

JOSEPH: That guy works, no matter what the job, eight bucks, twenty bucks an hour it doesn't matter he does it better than anybody and there you go. His parents are from Saint Louis (a town in the province of New Brunswick), came here in nineteen sixty-uh I don't know, when we were little kids. Good guy. Family were all workers. Father worked at a furniture factory. Mother cleaned houses for the rich people on the hill (a section of the city). He is what you called motivated, not one of those who stayed home and collected unemployment.

This story of a motivated person shows many of the traits of Acadian-American workers at many levels. Working hard regardless of the task and the rate of pay is admired by the other members, and the same story about C.D. was retold in another group much in the same way. The fact that people can point to him and say this is a motivated person is evidence of coherence among the members. C.D. took initiative and maintained the hockey rink better than others had before him and after him. The rate of pay, or a role that others might see as below him, did not affect his way of working. In the other group someone explained that it did not matter what the job was because he was giving it his best and this is what a motivated person does. The concept of making the best of a situation is also present in this account. Another important rule of an Acadian story is present here. C.D. chose not to collect unemployment, but preferred to work at a job that did not pay as well as what he previously had earned. This may be related to the strong sense of independence that group members talk about as a part of being Acadian, and the idea that you do not seek help from public agencies and institutions. As indicated above, families teach that you do a task for yourself, and the consequence of doing for yourself is developing a sense of who you are. The reflexive force tells you that success is in what you are, and not what the job is.

Many of the stories described how the parents were motivated people who worked hard without an education or technical skill. When they emigrated to the United States, they were poor. Not only did they successfully provide for their family, but many of them purchased houses for their families as well. One member pointed out that this was remarkable given the financial constraints they lived under. The families were large by today's standards. Members felt this may be attributed to their belief in Roman Catholicism, which forbids birth control, and also that the family was central to their life and feelings of success. All of the participants came from families of four or more children, and these families were sustained in spite of their size. The prominent belief among Acadian Americans is that motivated people find a relative degree of financial success through their hard work and the ability to save money. They proudly pointed to the homes their parents were able to buy as evidence that working hard will bring you and your family pride. This success along with other features in the FCWc reaffirm working and living as a motivated person.

Parents as motivated persons were described as people that do not complain or feel sorry for themselves. It's remarkable that in spite of a long history of hardship there is a force that does not allow an Acadian American to feel self-pity. The story of C.D. may be interpreted as a story of loss from a traditional American perspective, but he did not outwardly show sorrow or regret. There appears to be no room for an outward display of the emotion of sorrow. There were few stories of people expressing sorrow or despair when it came to job loss, layoffs, or plant closings. The absence of stories of sorrow after a loss may be explained by the grammar of acting as a motivated person. Motivated people dedicate themselves and their energy into making the best of all situations, and doing things for self. A motivated person knows that work, whether it is done at home or in the workplace leads to fulfillment and reward. One of the members stated, "You just make the best of what life has given, because hard work will always get what you need." This logical force is strong and sustains stories of working hard.

Honesty and Pride as Features of Working

The terms *honesty* and *pride* came up regularly in the interviews as part of the grammar of motivated persons. A motivated person is seen as an honest person, and they have pride in what they do and who they are. Honesty means that you are always truthful, and also that you give your employer an honest day's work. Participants feel that working hard is synonymous with honesty because you are honest with yourself, your employer, and your family by working as hard as you can and to a high level of expectation. The findings here would also suggest that you are honest to your community and religion as well. Participants did not clearly describe the obligation to give an employer an honest day's work. When asked where the level of work expectation comes from, members responded that it comes from within you, but you have heard it at home, in school, and in church, and you learn that this is that way to work.

The moral order of an honest day's work means doing the best you can even if no one notices. In the following, two members talk about what they experience if they are not able to give their best to a task:

RENE: I get through but I feel guilty. I got through it, but I want to push it out of my mind, not dwell on it. I feel a little panic actually. Knowing it's done but it was bad.

PAUL: In my job if you don't do your best the consequences are bad, but there are things you can't control. You have to learn not to make the same mistake twice, and it reflects so badly on you.

RENE: As a software engineer I can hide my mistakes and no one will know for five years if ever, because the program will work. It may not be the best way to make it work, but it works. I want it to work differently, perfectly. Sometimes I am told you only have so much time to get a project to work, and I am told to get it done. I <u>NEVER</u> want to see that project again because I know it's not the best work I can do. This is so hard for me. B::ut I work with many people who that's OK with, and they annoy me. In a big company like the one I am with you can get away with that your entire career, but put them in a small company and they will be exposed. You know who you can work with.

This section of a transcript illustrates the feelings that result from not doing a job as well as a person is capable of. Even though Rene may be directed to do less than his best, and even though it may be years before anyone would even notice, there is still a strong prefigurative force to work hard at the job and perform to a level of high expectation. Rene was emphatic that when he is prevented from doing that he wants to leave that experience behind when it is completed. He also states a feeling of annoyance with people who consistently work at levels less than what he feels should be accomplished. What is shown in this section is that a motivated person is internally motivated when performing a task, and must be honest with himself to feel a sense of accomplishment. Much like the story of C.D. who works at a high level of performance regardless of the pay or status of the job, Rene is concerned with working as a motivated person should. Pride is also apparent in these stories. When people are honest and give the best effort they can, they experience an emotion of pride. Members stated that pride comes from knowing that the job you finished, at home or at work, reflects who you are, and if it is done well you can take pride in its accomplishment. As we see in Rene's story, when it is not done well you want to forget about it, and may experience feelings of guilt or disappointment. From the interviews it appears that the autobiography of the Acadian Americans contains a strong obligation to act as a motivated person who must be honest and works toward attaining a sense of pride. Pride shows up in many ways in the stories of Acadian Americans. As discussed above, families take a great deal of pride in retelling stories of how others recognize a member of their family member as hard working. There is a strong sense of independence that is maintained by working hard, and not taking assistance from public agencies. As was shown, giving help has to follow a certain practice not to offend the receiving person's sense of pride and independence. Pride in this instance is an aspect of the aesthetic of work that Acadian Americans derive from working hard and being honest.

An Episode of a Motivated Person

One of the members spoke of an episode where he supervised one Acadian-American worker and several non-Acadian workers. He described the difference in rules that were in effect.

JOSEPH: The best case of this I ever saw was when I hired this guy right here from town to work where I work now. We are a bunch of techs that do installations, and troubleshoot for big computer systems. Every morning I bring the guys together, tell them what has got to get done for the day, who is going where, you know kind of like planning. After we meet we go down the street to Dunkin' Donuts for coffee, bring it back, and start the day. The first day I bring this French guy (Acadian American) in from Gardner. We go through the meeting, and this other guy says to him you can ride with us to get coffee. He says no I am all set, no thanks. When we get back, he's vacuuming the rugs in the office, which were a mess. The guys look at me. This goes on for several days and one morning the same guy (who offered the ride) says to him I am confused. Are you a technician or a janitor? He tells the guy the place is a mess; I am just doing my job.

CHARLIE: Figures . . . I know who you are talking about. Damn guys.

JOSEPH: But see it's more than that. I realize I never have to tell this guy a thing. He knows what to do next. It could be vacuuming, or computer work, he just knows, he gets it. He never has to be told what to do and he will do anything to get the job done.

MARIE: Oh yeah I know, I know.

JOSEPH: I told my boss if I could hire five Acadian guys I could make this company a million bucks more than it usually does.

CLAIRE: Hey that's no secret. The factories in this town made millions because of our mothers and fathers, and left them with nothing

At the heart of a CMM analysis is the question of how people tell stories and live stories, and how these stories are grammatically connected to other stories. CMM always comes back to action that sustains stories. In this episode, there is a connection between action and what it means to be a motivated person or a hard-working person. Here actions and feelings are enacted in a certain way that is regarded as motivated. The rules for action inform this new technician what to do next. However, as we see here, not all people understand the rules the Acadian Americans live by—which has implications for how these relationships are managed. The new technician (an Acadian American) has a competence that is recognized by his Acadian-American supervisor. The new technician can act into stories with features the supervisor can recognize because these are what are called culture-bearing stories (Hall, 1992). Culture-bearing stories are stories in which culture is lived out, as we see in this episode. This story can be sharply contrasted with a story one of the participants related. She said her boss avoids her when she acts motivated. Her boss is not Acadian and her actions as a motivated person may have little coherence for him.

The regulative rules describe the forces in this episode. The non-Acadian worker initiates the interaction by saying "you can ride with us to get coffee." In that statement by the non-Acadian worker, we see the antecedent act of condition as the expectation that all will take a break before work begins. His was to speak with the new worker, and the anticipated consequence was to have the new worker respond positively by saying he would go along. The deontic operator for the first worker is legitimate in light of the fact this is a daily practice and how you act at work. The locus of position is I–you in second person. The expected consequence is that the Acadian American will join in and share in the camaraderie in the workplace. The interaction occurs within the non-Acadian worker's rules for working that are embedded in the context. The highest context is the cultural pattern and life story that defined how a relationship to work and people should go. The cultural pattern appears to be one of individualism that affects the way in which one works. The worker's autobiography is the next level of context. Within this autobiography work is regarded as a tool that allows you to earn money or other rewards. The relation to work and others serves as the next lowest levels of the context. This invitation to come along for coffee may be an invitation to the Acadian American to sustain the rules for working in this organization.

The Acadian American who is enacting a story of a motivated person sees the invitation as an invitation from an unmotivated person to loaf. The Acadian American has an autobiographical story to do this job right. The response to work that is embedded within FCWc defines who you are. Work is not a tool, as it is for the non-Acadian; work is who you are. The Acadian American sees a work place that is in a state of mess and needs someone to straighten it up (vacuum the floor). In the view of a motivated person this is not the time to take a break and go out for coffee. The deontic operator is one of very strong obligation. The Acadian American acts with the expected consequence that he will be left alone to finish the work. The Acadian American's locus of position is me–to work as this messy workplace is overwhelming to him.

The non-Acadian worker experiences the declined invitation as a rejection; he may have been angered by it. Several days later he finds the new worker vacuuming the floor. The action of vacuuming is a surprise to all of the workers there, except for the supervisor, who understands it as typical of Acadians (like himself). The non-Acadian worker sees this as a puzzling event, not consistent with the way other technicians work in this place. The episode is not completed until the last interaction, when the employee states that he his confused and asks the new technician if he is a technician or a janitor. The employee is well aware that the Acadian-American worker is not a janitor, but offers this statement as a commentary about the way the new technician is working. The statement is offered with the expected consequence of changing the Acadian American's behavior and role at work.

The Acadian American calls upon rules that inform him that a "messy place" implies a responsibility to act as a motivated person would act, and clean it. There is a logical force that sees this action as making sense in the workplace for him, and this action reaffirms his selfhood. He probably recognizes that others will see this as unusual behavior, but the practical force of how others see it, and the employee's questions are weak practical forces. He goes ahead and acts out a story of a motivated person. The Acadian American bears a force that is internal, but is connected to FCWc. He has learned a feeling when things in the environment are in a certain condition he must act to correct it no matter how that may look to others present. When the Acadian American hears the question, he recognizes it is the time to act a story of conciliation so he may be left alone to do his work. Conciliation is a way of addressing the threats from others who rely upon different rules for action. The Acadian American recognizes that he has encountered someone who does not understand how to work. His ideas of working come from experiences in FCWc and may differ significantly from the non-Acadian worker. The consequence for him is to work hard which is consistent with a deontic operator that is obligatory which comes from the FCWc pattern of working hard and acting as a motivated person. The autobiographies for both of these workers differ in how one acts at work, and what constitutes being "motivated." For the Acadian American, choosing to vacuum the floor, rather than going out for coffee is further evidence of successful enactment of what you are about. The task at hand, in this case vacuuming, is not as critical as working as a motivated person would work, which is to do all things that need to be done. The reflexive need is to work hard no matter what the task and this action will reconstitute what being an Acadian American is all about.

The supervisor's response further affirms action as a "motivated person." The supervisor values a worker who can anticipate what to do, needs little direction, and acts as a motivated person would act. Later in the transcript, the supervisor states that if he had more Acadian workers he could make more money for the company. This statement shows a level of coherence between him and the Acadian worker, and that work in this way satisfies a reflexive need to extend stories of how people should work for a supervisor.

Aesthetics of Working

Members talked about a feeling that accompanies episodes of working hard, or working as a motivated person would. This aesthetic dimension of working is explored here. The feeling of working hard is a meaningful aspect of the grammar of working. The feeling extends beyond words that can describe what working hard is like. There is a physical feeling that is part of everyday practice and cannot be separated from language, yet it is never fully captured in words. Workers discussed that they know how to work and can tell when they have worked hard by the feeling that comes over them. It is in these kinds of statements that aesthetics are found in lived experience. In the interviews there was evidence of members sharing common understandings of what this grammar of working hard feels like. These portions from the transcript illustrate the members" aesthetic experience:

INTERVIEWER: *Earlier you had mentioned that working hard has a feeling. Could you describe that feeling?*

THERESA: It's feeling proud[

JOAN: [Oh that's what it is. You feel so proud you stand there and say I did it[

THERESA: [Total satisfaction[

JOAN: [Total satisfaction. Total! Oh don't you feel good?

LINDA: It's a physical and emotional feeling, even a little euphoria. You may feel exhausted but it feels so good. Kind of like a rush, it's so worth it.

JOAN: Yes! Yes!

LINDA: I feel it in my head; no it's just too good!

JOAN: At home OH! [

LINDA: [If you work really hard at home, or at work it doesn't matter. It feels so good.

INTERVIEWER: *Does this feeling happen more often at home or work?*

DORIS: About the same . . . I don't know. I like feeling good about something that happened for the rest of the day.

LINDA: Yes, feeling good for the rest of the day.

THERESA: It's the same in both places for me.

INTERVIEWER: *How do you express it?*

DORIS: You want to yell, Yes!

JOAN: Don't you feel that is better than the people who are just whining?

DORIS: Yeah, I do.

In another group it was the aesthetic of working hard that was expressed in this way:

PAUL: Just this week we had to manage a big project at work. It was a lot of work. We had to coordinate with people all over the state. It came off beautifully. When it was done, I just stood back and said to myself, this is great. This is what I work for. This feeling of accomplishment, and knowing I did my best and it all worked. I felt so good.

The members in the interviews clearly knew what this feeling was, and they extended each other's stories with reflexive effects. It was described in slightly different terms such as "euphoria, a rush, total satisfaction, or a sense of accomplishment," but clearly all shared an understanding of what this was. There was a positive aesthetic for hard work, just as there were feelings of dissatisfaction as seen in the episodes of people who did not work as hard or as well as they might have. Making sense of the aesthetics of working helps in understanding the grammar of working. The rules and grammars of working are not individual matters, and neither are the feelings associated with working hard that the members experience. Evidence of the grammar of working is found in the mutual understanding of these feelings as members talk about them in the transcript. The fact that there is mutual awareness indicates that there are levels of coherence and coordination among them. The interruptions in the first section of transcript are offered as confirmation, and a desire to extend the story of feelings about working hard. These exchanges also point to the idea that feelings included in the grammar of working are a socially shared phenomenon and not a singular experience. The rules for telling the story of an intense feeling with regard to work are widely available as well as recognized by all of the members who were interviewed.

Cronen and Lang (1994) described a grammar of emotion is coupled with a grammar of expression to form a unity as was seen here. The feeling and its expression are vital features of the grammar of working. As Cronen and Lang described, the members have learned how to have these emotions under particular circumstances and have also learned how to enact these emotions and express them. This expression and practice of feeling about work has been learned within FCWc. Knowing the rules of working hard within FCWc is not enough to be a member of the community. A member must be able to work hard and to feel and express this pattern of action.

Feelings indicate to the members if an episode of working is going well or not. The feelings are a measure of achievement of the prefigurative forces found in the FCWc that are constitutive for the members. This feeling was known to Paul who described feelings of accomplishment in the transcript above, as well as it was to the other members. Members were asked, whose voice do you hear when you work the right way or you don't work as hard as you could have. The answers came back; those of the people in FCWc, such as parents, teachers, and priests. The members identified people from their family, church or school as the voices that tell them when they are doing a good job.

Actions and the feelings that come with working hard emanate from the rules and forces that are found within FCWc. The rules are not individually held or constructed. The feelings that come from working, or following the rules, are a shared and common understanding that provides a heightened sense of identity and membership in a community. The emotional content of working hard may be produced and felt by individuals, but there is a relationship with the community itself. Once again calling on Dewey's idea, experiences may be produced and enjoyed by individuals, but they become what they are within the context of their experience because of the culture in which people participate. Awareness of the rules of working hard is not enough. Members must act in certain ways and feel a certain way to achieve coherence with FCWc. There are similar features described, such as its engrossing nature, and there is evidence of a shared understanding of this. This common understanding was seen in the first transcript when members interjected their own descriptions to the others in a spirit of affirmation and understanding.

The aesthetics of work serves as a strong force that moves the members to act an Acadian story of work and selfhood.

Making a Difference

The participants discussed the way they work both at home and at their job as working as hard as they could, and doing the best job possible. When asked what kind of person does it make you if you work hard, a common response was given with just slight variations among the groups interviewed, this next section of transcript is indicative of the kind of response that was given to the question.

INTERVIEWER: *What kind of person does it make you if you work hard?*

LINDA: An honorable person, honest person[

JOAN: [YES! YES!

Theresa: You feel good about yourself. A good day at work, you go home feeling this was a good day. It doesn't matter how busy it was.

JOAN: But you feel like you are helping the family with the, um, financial part whatever you are doing[

LINDA: [You feel worthy[

JOAN: [YES!

LINDA: You also feel that if you have done something well you have made a difference in someone's life no matter what it is.

DORIS: Very well put Linda! That is exactly it.

LINDA: That's right. If it's in an office it doesn't matter, a hospital, school, a classroom, wherever, you are making a difference in somebody's life.

INTERVIEWER: *When you say difference, what do you think of?*

LINDA: You reached out, maybe answered a question, or helped somebody, directed them to the right thing. Send them the right way. It doesn't even have to be that deep. Somebody is having a bad day, like little children that would come into the hospital and I would say you are having a sad day, and I would sit and hold them or hold their hand. Just having someone there.

INTERVIEWER: *So can you make a difference in people's lives by all kinds of jobs?*

JOAN: Yes, if I was at Walmart and a woman was upset. I could help[

LINDA: [No matter where you are you can make a

difference in someone's life. No matter where you.

DORIS: Even just opening the door for someone[

THERESA: [Or taking a minute.

INTERVIEWER: *What tells you that you should be making a difference?*

LINDA: We saw our parents do it[

THERESA: [We were raised that way[

JOAN: [You were raised that way, thankful for what you had, and if somebody has less than you, you help.

THERESA: There is the religion part too.

JOAN: Absolutely!

DORIS: Having been brought up in a parochial school[

JOAN: [And you just always helped when you can. If you are not in the situation, you are just glad that you are not.

THERESA: Mmm, you care.

JOAN: I feel for that other person

LINDA: But you have some pretty heavy morals[

JOAN: [Oh big time morals[

LINDA: [Right from day one it's drilled into you.

Members of a nonprofessional group answered the question of what kind of person it makes you if you work hard in this way:

MARIE: I work assembling fire alarms. I know when I put the finished piece in the box it could save someone's life. My hard work makes the world a little better, could save a life.

CLAIRE: I have always felt the same way. If I work harder, somebody's life could be saved, or be made better, and the world is a better place. Even something as small as making a fire alarm, helping out at a school function, anything.

MARIE: I feel lucky to be able to help out and give something. It's more than a paycheck to me. Ever since I was little, I wanted a job helping out and I guess I have one.

CLAIRE: I think we do, and I feel proud of it

There is a strong moral force to give to others, or to the community at large. The first group of people were professionals that have daily contact with people as part of their job, and the second group were two people who work in a factory, far from direct contact with the public. However, both have a desire to contribute to the well-being of others. The members attribute this to a religious foundation, taught in church and school, as well as what they saw their parents do. While these concepts may have been taught within the family, church, or school, members continue to enact these expectations in all kinds of jobs. Jobs in a factory, assembling a piece of machinery, or jobs in a retail store are linked to this moral foundation. Work is a part of the life a good person lives, and by working hard a good person reaffirms an Acadian story of how to live and work. Working to make a difference in someone else's life is a different kind of reason for working from accumulating wealth, or working just for the money. Working serves an obligation to take care of family, but also an obligation to make a difference in your community. Making a difference is a moral force that helps to understand how work for Acadian Americans is enacted in a particular way. There are stories of people working hard at menial jobs, or tasks at home. Working, no matter in what context, must go a certain way, and Acadians must work to do the best they can for others. In the process of making a difference, their own selfhood is reaffirmed as they are living according to the logical forces in FCWc.

There are no distinctions made by the members between working to make a difference for people of your culture or others cultures, in fact the people in these interviews would have come into contact with people of many backgrounds. Work must be done well to help all people.

There is also an aesthetic dimension to making a difference that the members responded to in the interviews. Note when Linda made her statement, Doris followed with a strong comment that what Linda had said was very well put. The other members followed with comments extending the concept of making a difference, indicating a level of understanding about what it is to make a difference. This understanding was expressed by the members through kinesic and vocalic features that the transcript cannot adequately represent. The members became very intense and active at this point in the interview. The transcript does show the amount of interruption, which attests to the level of activity in contributing in this conjoint story. There are reflexive effects present when the members are sharing in a story of what a person is, and should do to make a difference in others' lives. The statement of making a difference receives

Doris's response and the comments of the other members. The stories of making a difference continue in a conjoint process that expands Linda's statement into actions and instances of making a difference such as holding a hand, opening a door, assisting a distressed customer, or taking a minute. These are all actions a good person performs, and each one of these actions was offered by a different member to enlarge the concept initially offered by Linda.

A similar occurrence happens in the second group when Marie talks of feeling that she can make the world a little better through her work, and Claire extends the story. Again, there was a sense of obligation to the larger community, and working for more than just money. Marie and Claire expressed this sentiment with a depth that showed an appreciation or feel for making a difference. This exchange had a level of meaning and sincerity for both members. They expressed that work means more than just a set of tasks. Working is a way to live a life as a good person should. Again, there is a weaving of family obligations, cultural forces, and religious principals into the action of working. Working hard, and working to make a difference is what a person must and should do.

There is a reflexive need to work and to work to make a difference. The agreement and shared sense of making a difference for others was important to these members. This is a way an Acadian belongs to their community and fits with other members in living a life that is coherent.

However, the aesthetics of making a difference should not be overlooked. It is within the feelings and the actions of lived experience of making a difference that Acadian Americans know they are living an Acadian story and working in the way that they must work. There is a feeling dimension about making a difference that represents the beautiful fit Dewey spoke of when things come together, but are not capable of being expressed in words (Dewey, 1934). The shared feelings expressed in the transcript partially in words, and partially in the action, magnifies the sense of identity and belonging the members have with their community. Within their community, people experience work in a certain way and part of that experience is feelings that organize and symbolize the experience in a meaningful way. The feelings associated with working are a significant aspect of the grammar of working. The aesthetic of making a difference also enriches an understanding of the grammar of working and provide an opportunity to understand what meanings are informing their behaviors.

Chapter 8

Life Outside the Community

THE ACADIAN AMERICANS PARTICIPATE in the larger American communities as workers, neighbors, consumers, and in all of the social roles that life demands. This is not a community that can isolate itself, nor does it want to. However, Acadian Americans share common stories about how episodes of living should be enacted. In this chapter the major stories of how life should be lived from an Acadian American perspective are focused on working, honesty, financial debt, and the frustrations they feel with people who do not share their ideas about these concepts. Again there are strong moral influences from their Catholicism and a common story of how to manage interpersonal encounters when dealing with non-Acadians. All of the interviewees expressed similar concerns with the people and situations they encountered outside of their cultural frame.

It appeared that in the work setting Acadian Americans talk about people as being motivated or non-motivated. They often spoke of the differences between motivated and non-motivated people. Earlier, Rene made a statement about other engineers that is indicative of stories that were related about workers. When asked what it is like to work with people who don't work in the same ways that Acadian Americans do, the answers were very definite that there are too many people that do not work as hard or in the same way. This was reported as mostly likely to occur with non-Acadian people. In this exchange group members are discussing people they work with at their jobs:

JOAN: It annoys me when I hear people whine all day and you never hear that from an Acadian. I want to say SHUT-UP!, Stop your friggin' whining. You are not the only one who has kids to take care of, but God they whine all the time. Whine, whine, whine.

DORIS: I find it annoying, and it happens a lot, when I put in a lot of hours on a school wide project and I went to the library, got tons of information, ran around, and people have not done a DAMN THING yet and here I am[

LINDA: [and those are always the biggest complainers.

DORIS: Yes you are right and that annoys me. I find myself trying to do it, in a teasing way but I bet I get my boss mad. There are days when I want to light a fire under him and say <u>CAN'T YOU GET MOVING?</u> Geez! I did this and this last night and the guy who is like ten years older than me, and is the boss . . . and it's like, <u>GOD!</u> Do something extra, or do what you have to.

INTERVIEWER: *How does your boss respond to you when you say things in a teasing way, or show you are annoyed?*

LINDA: Oh God you never say these things, you feel them and do a little extra.

DORIS: No, you can't say them. I know I am there to do a good job not to boss him around, but there are times when he does avoid me[

LINDA: [anything to the other teachers?

DORIS: No, I would never, that is not my way.

The participants understood each other and shared this feeling of being annoyed with people who were not motivated. This theme came up in all of the interviews. Although it is permissible to feel annoyed (a term used by Doris and by Rene) when working with others who are not motivated, Acadian Americans report a deontic operator of being prohibited from saying anything, or even talking to others about this experience. Participants related stories of their parents in the work place who came up against these same challenges. The usual way their parents would handle these difficulties was to avoid saying anything to the person who was not working hard. Parents would share these stories with their family, but at work they would make up the difference in terms of work output, and never complain. This action is consistent with the forces of not complaining which is a central feature of selfhood in the Acadian American community. All of the participants expressed feeling annoyed with people who were not motivated. They went on to say they do their job, but not say anything about the person who doesn't work. However, the members did share these stories freely among themselves in the interviews. At the end of one of the group interviews this exchange took place among the participants:

JOAN: I have to go and get supper ready. Then work tomorrow, that woman next to me I have to get ready to hear her whine. I want to say you think you are the only one who works. <u>SHUT UP! OH I CAN'T HANDLE IT!</u> Stop whining and just do what you are paid to do, because we are getting nowhere. Your whining has cost us a half hour and we could have been six pages ahead now. They do poor poor me. They say I have to bring my kid, and I say yeah, but inside I want to say I do it every day so <u>SHUT UP!</u> Keep moving. Look at that poutine woman she is 93, still rolling[(refers to the annual church fair and a woman who volunteers each day of the fair to make an Acadian potato dish)

THERESA: People, I tell you they work so hard[

JOAN: [and you don't hear them whine[

THERESA: [They work hard[

JOAN: [Exactly[

DORIS: [They have fun[

JOAN: [Look at your mother (to Doris); she is there every year you never hear her say WAA-WAA-WAA! Like those idiots I work with.

DORIS: My mother talks about it all the time, how she works five days straight at the fair making poutines. [

LINDA: [They are used to hard work and the women are used to working around food. It's a big thing in their life and then they go to the fair and they are with all the people from their own background.

JOAN: But they don't want no thank-yous. Never complain. Never asked for a thank-you. Never hear your mother say you kids don't appreciate nothing ever. You know what she gets such enjoyment out of doing it for us that it didn't matter. She did it for herself too. As we grew up, I said mom, we were terrible the nights we came in when you made those nice meals and we would bitch because you asked for help with the dishes. You didn't realize that she was doing so much.

THERESA: No, you don't.

JOAN: I use to leave her there with dishes or be upset when she made me do the dishes, and she never complained.

In this exchange the actions of the parents, both in the present and the past, are used to reaffirm the rules of working hard, and not complaining or feeling sorry for yourself. The frustration with other kinds of workers is clear, but the force of not expressing how annoyed you are is also strong. In the other interviews many of the participants express the idea that if people "kept moving" and "worked instead of whining the job would get done." The whining and complaining are regarded as wasted energy, because they violate the logical forces of working as a motivated person would. The forces that compel Acadian Americans to work are much different from the forces that affect most other people they come into contact with.

A statement made by Claire in the transcript quoted in chapter 7, which described an episode of the Acadian-American computer technician points to a tension that exists between Acadian Americans and non-Acadians.

JOSEPH: I told my boss if I could hire five Acadian guys I could make this company a million bucks more than it usually does.

CLAIRE: Hey that's no secret. The factories in this town made millions because of our mothers and fathers, and left them with nothing

Claire recognizes that hard-working Acadians have received little in the way of financial compensation and recognition. As seen in the episode of the technician who vacuums the floor, there appears to be little understanding on the part of outsiders of Acadian Americans who work in this way. There is an underlying theme in the interviews of tension, frustration, and annoyance with non-Acadians. The frustration is not targeted at the lack of earnings. Low wages are reconciled by a story that you make the best of what life gives you. The tension is focused on stories of people not working hard, complaining, and not making the best of what is. The tension is felt toward those whose beliefs are in strong opposition to the moral orders, rules, and forces implicit in FCWc.

The Impossibility of Managing Others

A common finding was the lack of Acadian Americans who seek management positions. Few of the participants had jobs with supervisory responsibilities. When asked about this, the common response was that there is no desire to be a boss at work. The reasons for this included: too many headaches in managing others, feeling they were not the best leader, or feeling satisfied with where they were. One participant owns his own business, but stated it's a small family business that he runs with his father and a few part-time workers. The only participant who was a manager described his job as frustrating because it was hard for him to get people to work the way he does. This is the same person who stated if he had five Acadian workers he could make a company a million dollars more. Acadian Americans are often recognized as hard workers by others outside of their culture, and usually the most effective workers are promoted. When a question was directed to the participants about being offered management positions, most responded that they could have become a manager, but they either dismissed peoples' encouragement to become a manager, or they avoided the role by not seeking promotions.

When asked, if a motivated person is expected to take charge, how is it that a motivated person avoids the responsibility of managing? the response was that taking charge as a motivated person is different from being a manager. A manager is someone that has to direct and stand apart from workers, and that is not what these members would want to do. The general consensus was that most managers are too far away from the work itself. Both the professional and non-professional participants thought that managers spend too much time talking in meetings and not doing a "real" job. Participants expressed that management is not hands-on enough, there are a lack of tasks, and also that management is too stressful. Participants saw differences between leading others at work and leading members of your culture in a church project or a community project. In both the larger community and at work they were not as likely to assume responsibility for directing others as they would if they were in their own community or at home. One member related a story of working on a committee for a youth organization. She stated she found it easier to do all of the committee's work rather than trying to lead others, as she related this story other members reported similar experiences. Here a motivated person must act alone and finish the tasks that others are likely to complain about, or not address as an Acadian American would.

Fulfilling the role of a manager, and acting as motivated person, could lead to overwhelming self-expectations. A motivated person must complete the work that others do not complete, and organizations are made up of many kinds of people, who may work in many different ways. The members described feelings of annoyance with people outside their community because they do not work in a manner similar to them. A motivated person, and manager, would be responsible for finishing everyone's work, including those people who do not have the same forces for working. As we have seen, a motivated person does not complain and completes the work for a co-worker. Being a manager would make a motivated person responsible for everyone under the manager's supervision. This overpowering level of responsibility would be added to feeling annoyed with these individuals. Within the Acadian-American community, there is less of a risk in assuming responsibility for others because of the common expectations, and forces of the FCWc. It is reasonable to expect that other Acadian Americans will work in much the same way as the motivated person who is directing them. However, outside of the Acadian-American community many things could go differently because people are likely to live by forces that differ from the forces Acadians live by.

Two participants recounted that they had once worked together at an assembly task in a factory, and there was a company initiative to increase productivity. They thought if they could set an example by working hard others would follow. They would encourage others to work harder, but said it only lead to more frustration and the feeling that these people didn't understand what hard work was. One of the participants said that this experience told her she was not "cut out" to be a manager. She stated she could not get through to these people, and found herself getting frustrated. Again there is evidence of a sense of selfhood derived from work and the position that the "motivated" person takes in the work place. The relationship is between the person and the task. A sense of satisfaction or completion comes from a prefigurative force that directs a person to work in a certain way. It may be difficult to understand someone who does not have the same logical forces for working, which would make management a daunting task. Directing others is not necessary within an Acadian American way of working because working hard is directed by prefigurative forces.

Managing others is also made difficult because of the conciliatory nature of interpersonal relationships. The expectation for working is to finish a job or a task, and if necessary finish the work of someone who has not finished his or her work. Confrontation with someone who is not doing his or her job is avoided. The deontic operator here is prohibition. However, it is legitimate to experience feelings of annoyance with others who do not work hard. Managing others has the potential to breach the conciliatory stance in interpersonal relationships because a manager would have to direct, and possibly confront a non-Acadian American. This is not to say that there are no Acadian Americans who have taken on supervisory responsibilities. Among the participants in the interviews, there were two individuals who have supervised others. One managed people in a small business that he co-owns with a family member. The other member has managed successfully at several different organizations and mostly non-Acadian people; however, as seen earlier, he does make the comment that Acadian Americans know how to work and are more productive.

The discussion in one of the groups produced a consensus that managing people who don't work hard would be difficult, and there was agreement that most people do not work to the expectations of most Acadian Americans. One of the participants who works as a nurse stated that she has seen other people who are not Acadian Americans work very hard, but it's not as likely as when she has worked with other Acadian Americans. In her experience, the Acadian Americans work harder, assume more responsibility, and never complain or question supervisors. She related the story of the housekeeper who works on her floor in the hospital who came from New Brunswick in the 1950s. The housekeeper is seventy-three years old and does not want to retire. The floor is still the best-kept floor in the hospital and other nurses and physicians will comment on how clean and organized the unit is. The housekeeper was described as a "motivated" person who takes great pride in her work. The other nurses on the floor recognized her by naming her an honorary registered nurse. The participant went on to say that this had not been her experience with other housekeepers. The other housekeepers lacked ambition, and seemed to want to get out of work rather than do it. This member stated that people's attitudes toward work is one of the things that tells her that management is not for her.

Owing Money

In all of the interviews the members discussed the importance of not owing money to others. With the exception of a mortgage on a home, or a loan to buy a car, members were clear that owing money is not a position they want to be in. In these sections of transcripts this theme is explored.

INTERVIEWER: *You had mentioned before that it is important to not owe any money to anyone. If you did owe money what would some of your concerns be?*

CLAIRE: It would never happen. I seldom use a credit card, and if I do I pay right a way. They never make money on me.

CHARLIE: I pay right away too. If I can't afford it, DON'T BUY IT!

INTERVIEWER: *Do you think that is an Acadian trait, or are there other people like that?*

MARIE: Yes—you don't owe anyone, that's Acadian. I don't owe anyone. Like all my girlfriends who are not Acadian talk about their maxed-out credit cards[

JOSEPH: [I never had a late bill in my life[

CLAIRE: [Me neither, or my parents. That would be hard to live with.

INTERVIEWER: *What would happen if you did owe money?*

CLAIRE: I just wouldn't want it[

MARIE: [I would be embarrassed and feel like a deadbeat.

CLAIRE: I couldn't even tell you what it would be like. Both me and my husband grew up in families that really watched their money. They built their house when they had the money, they would put a room in when they had the cash, never borrow. My brother did the same thing, built a beautiful house but lived with plywood floors and sheet rock walls until he had the money. We don't do anything until we have the money. You don't want to get in debt.

MARIE: You don't want to owe anybody, the only two things you are allowed in life to owe money on are a house and car only because they got so damn expensive.

CLAIRE: That's right and you avoid those if you can.

MARIE: I agree

JOSEPH: You find more French guys in this town who build houses do it like that. (pause) A room at a time. Frame the room first, then add the sheet rock, floor piece by piece all cash. It's theirs when it's done, nobody else's.

INTERVIEWER: *What would happen if you owed money to people, or to a bank, or a business?*

CLAIRE: If you owe they have something on you.

(long silence)

INTERVIEWER: *What would they have?*

CLAIRE: I just don't want anyone to have anything on me[

MARIE: [I work hard and I am not going to give my money away.

JOSEPH: People talk about credit cards and percentages, I say what are percentages? Percent, hmm, I don't owe anyone. I don't have a balance anywhere.

CLAIRE: Me too. We have one (referring to credit card), never carried a balance to the next month.

CHARLIE: I was late one time on my car payment. My father had died and I forgot to pay it when I got back I found it so I wrote them a letter apologizing.

One day I got a letter from the bank saying I was late. I said Oh Man! So I wrote a letter saying I was so sorry.

INTERVIEWER: *What happened then?*

CHARLIE: Nothing happened they didn't care but it was just me. I made that bill. I owe that money. I don't want them to think I am like that. I owe the money, and I will make it good.

MARIE: I was late on a bill once, a car payment. I went to see the loan officer and I apologized to her. She kept telling me it was OK (laughs). I was a wreck, that will never happen again.

INTERVIEWER: *Were your parents like this?*

MARIE: Oh they never owed anybody for anything, and they lived within their means.

JOSEPH: One of my sons is really into music. There was a sale at the music store. He wanted something for his guitar. He had $90 in his pocket that took him a long time to save. He walked into the store thinking the item was half price but the sign said up to 50% off and this item was not one of them. It would cost $120. He looked at me, and I said I am not giving you the money. He almost cried in the store, the man asked if there was a problem and I said he doesn't have the money yet. The man said I will keep the sale on for a while longer. I told him it would be more than a little while because I am not going to do that. You have to save and go in and buy it. That's what it's all about.

INTERVIEWER: *What does it mean when you say, "that's what it's all about?"*

MARIE: I have to say when I bought my first junk car I did it on my own. It was very important—you have to do that. That's the work ethic. That's why, that's how you teach your kids, you want something in life you have to work and save, you have to work for it.

CLAIRE: You saved and when you have that money what a good feeling that is. I did it myself.

JOSEPH: When I say, that's what it's all about I mean it's you. You did it.

The conversants share an understanding and a common story of the importance of not owing money. While at times they did not clearly articulate the significance of this, it seemed clear that they shared a common understanding of the reasons for not owing money, and that it's much more desirable to get what you want through having completely earned it by work, and not credit. The feeling that comes from owing money is an important aspect of the grammar of owing. Owing money is associated with feelings that Marie describes as embarrassment, or being a deadbeat. Owing money brings about feelings similar to those that come from accepting public charity or a gift from a neighbor. Accepting and owing both violate logical forces that make an Acadian American "do it for yourself." Not taking or borrowing may mean going without things you may want, as seen in the case of Claire's brother and in-laws who built their houses as they had the cash, or Joseph's son who wanted the item in the music store. These members saw parents who lived within their means, and seldom borrowed money. Joseph's story said that his son had to learn a lesson about living without things you want; this will make you a better person, and you remain faithful to forces that tell you to do it for yourself. Marie related the story of buying her first "junk car" as important, something you must do. Marie goes on to say that this is the work ethic, and the work ethic is something you must teach your kids. The grammar of the work ethic includes the capability to work, save money, and buy things with your own money. All things can come to you through hard work. Working makes a person independent, a person who does it for herself or himself. Again, the concepts of FCWc are entwined and work is a critical feature of living an Acadian story. It is through work that you are able to become a good person, and act as an Acadian American should act.

Living without the things you want is tolerable when you make the best of a situation—which is learning to feel satisfaction with meeting moral forces, and not in accumulating possessions. The signs of success are not found in the things you own. Success is found in family, and community relationships, and how closely you can follow the prefigurative forces that are developed through working, family, culture, and church. These forces include common understandings of doing it for yourself, making a difference, being honest, and working as a motivated person. Living as a good person is a better sign of success for Acadian Americans than living as a person who has many things and objects. Owing money to others contradicts the logical forces that tell an Acadian American how to live a good life.

There are no explicit answers offered by the members about what it is that people would "have on you" if you owed money. However, the way the members extend the stories and each participates in relating episodes about not owing indicates that they share a common understanding of what it means not to owe money.

Reconciliation

Owing money may not be as much an issue of others having control over you as an individual moral issue. Charlie's story of being late with a payment to the bank indicates these forces and how strong they are in living a life. Charlie was aware that the consequences from the bank were not going to be serious or jeopardize his credit, yet he was compelled to write a letter of apology. Marie relates a similar story and talks about being upset about the incident and needing to apologize for this. Within these episodes there is evidence of moral forces, and religious teaching effecting selfhood. Charlie's and Marie's actions mirror the Catholic sacrament of penance. The sacrament offers mercy and pardon for having offended God, and at the same time offers reconciliation with the church or your community. The Catholic Church views every sin as an offence against God that disrupts a relationship between God and the person. It is through penance that Catholics may love God deeply and commit themselves completely. In the view of the Church, penance always requires reconciliation with all people within the church community. The most important act of the penitent is contrition, a deep sorrow and repulsion of the sin with the intention of sinning no more. It is believed that heaven and the kingdom of Christ is made possible by metanoia, a profound change of the person where their life is considered, judged, and arranged according to the holiness and love of God. However, the genuineness of penance is weighed against a deeply felt contrition. The conversion should affect a person and move them toward a progressively deeper enlightenment and closer relationship to Christ. An outward accusation must be made in light of God's mercy. Confession requires that the penitent address the minister of God, and the minister of God acting in the person of Christ pronounces a decision of forgiveness or retention of sins. The sacrament entails expiation for the sins committed, amendment of a life, and rectifying injuries done. Through penance the person may restore the order they have upset, and be cured of the transgression they committed. Penance is a remedy for sin and a help to renewal of life. The Church does not see this as a ritual repetition but an effort to perfect the grace of baptism (Remy, 1910).

It may be said Charlie's letter to the bank and Marie's apology share many of the moral forces that are found in the sacrament of Penance. His writing a letter, and her apology, as well as "being a wreck," demonstrated how deeply they felt about this oversight. A late payment or forgetting about paying means they were not acting an Acadian American story of responsibility. A public statement to those in charge of the bank is much like a statement to a priest who acts on behalf of the church. Both Charlie's and Marie's violations were against the Acadian-American story of responsibility. Their failure to make the payment on time upset the order of what a good person does. An apology, or an act of contrition, to a person in charge, is analogous to a statement made to the church or community. Acadian Americans do not see distinct differences between FCWc. Therefore an action that violates moral forces requires an effort to seek reconciliation and begin a process to lead an amended life. When the members are able to recognize and admit their lapses toward the moral forces, they are able to move toward a deeper recognition of what a good person must do. Both Charlie and Marie spoke openly within the group about their failure to pay a bill on time; they did not keep this personal wrong a private matter. They reflected on the experience as an event that changed them, a lesson learned, and they will not violate this rule again. It may be said there is an enlightenment of sorts that will help them to live their lives in line with an Acadian-American story.

A Second Game

The discussion about dealing with people outside of their community revealed another episodic "game" that was played by the members. Usually the members would talk about an episode they were involved in outside of their community, such as at work. They would make a statement that they really didn't know much about it, that they were either "stupid" or "dumb." The others would laugh, which affirmed the statement, and the discussion would go on. Here is a section of transcript that is typical of this game:

CHARLIE: My boss comes up to me and says you have been here almost twenty years, what do you think we should do. I laughed and said hey don't ask me I am just a dumb Frenchman.

OTHERS: (Laugh)

CHARLIE: I figure he's the one who owns the place, let him make the decisions

Here is another example of the game being played:

LINDA: I tend not to get involved with things other than taking care of my patients at work. People love to talk about what is going on at work and they will look at me and say "You are quiet." I usually respond, "what do I know, I am not the smartest person in the hospital."

DORIS: It can be like that in town, too. Politics, whatever doesn't concern me. I don't have the mentality to deal with that stuff.

LINDA: I know what you mean. Leave it for the smart people.

DORIS: (Laughs) That's right, leave to the smarter people.

There are other times when talking with Acadian Americans I have heard comments similar to this. It may be attributed to forces that prohibit complaining, direct a person to make the best of what they have, and a way to manage interpersonal relationships. Assuming a standard of knowing also entails responsibilities of more interaction with others outside of the Acadian American community, and it changes the nature of interpersonal relationships that are based on appeasing others. A position of not knowing relieves a person of these responsibilities. Acadian Americans have been successful in many areas of life, and there is no evidence of them not being "smart enough" to accomplish whatever they care to undertake. The conversations about others reveal the members have definite opinions of non-Acadians. These opinions include commentary on performance, trust, honesty, and ability or willingness to work hard. Playing this game relieves the members of responsibilities and allows them to work more independently—in a way that is to do it for yourself. They will work as a motivated person, and give an honest day's work that satisfies a reflexive need to do it for yourself, and do the best they can for their employer. However there is a desire to stay away from relationships with people who do not have a similar sense of pride, do not work hard, or are prone to complaining. People such as this create annoyances. Playing this game, like shunning management positions, keeps the members out of relationships they are reluctant to enter into. They are able to successfully enact stories of how they should work, and manage life with people outside of their community.

When the game is played, both players know it is just a game. Both laugh at the game when it is played. For example, a member might say, it's just me being stupid again; both the person who said this and the person they are directing the comment to would laugh. The laughter serves in this case as affirmation of the game and not an affirmation of a lack of intelligence or common sense. In the episodes when the Acadian American talks about an exchange with a non-Acadian, laughter serves to inform the speaker that I understand what you are doing in that interaction.

Trading With Non-Acadians

We have said that trading with non-Acadians is difficult for the members. Members stated that going outside of their community made them vulnerable to others who may not be as honest. The majority of members related that they hire Acadian American contractors to repair, build, or renovate their houses. They will go to members of their own community for products and services that they need, even when it may mean spending more money. The members justified the expense by saying that they knew an Acadian would stand behind their work and be honest. The belief was that another Acadian American would work hard to do the best job possible. Members explained that this was much easier in the past because there were local merchants who were members of your community that you could go to. Now, many of the small local shops have closed and many purchases are now made in national retail outlets. One member stated that she recently bought a computer and she and her husband felt they were at the mercy of the salesperson whom they did not know. When asked how they purchase items such as computers, appliances, or cars, they responded that they seek the opinion of members of their community and listen to what they have to say. The members seek a base of experience from within their own community that can address issues such as honesty, and quality of a product of service. The communication between the Acadian Americans about products or services is critical, as the members share a common understanding about issues of honesty and quality.

One of the members spoke of the credit union that was established within the Acadian community and still exists today. This member's mother worked as a loan officer for the credit union, and he reported that she told him stories of how loans were extended to hard-working Acadians who would usually repay their loans ahead of time. He described the relationships between the loan officers and the families borrowing money to buy homes, or cars, or to start businesses. These relationships were an important part of doing business. The relationship between the credit union and the Acadian community was unlike relationships banks usually have with its customers. There was a strong sense of loyalty on both parties' parts and trust among members of the Acadian-American community that they would be treated fairly. This member explained that an Acadian would seldom borrow for "foolish" reasons, which is consistent with the forces that prohibit owing money. The credit union may be viewed as an institution that extended the dimensions of FCWc. It is located within close proximity of the church, and has employed bilingual Acadian-American staff and managers who are usually active members of the Acadian-American community. This financial institution understood the needs of its members and enacted business and professional relationships according to an Acadian story.

Trade and business transactions among the Acadian Americans also adhere to the strong logical forces of life within the community. Trade with people outside of the system may follow a different set of rules and forces. An Acadian American is likely to be prohibited from being confrontational with members of other communities and as a result are at the mercy of others. The grammar of "at the mercy of others" includes actions of not complaining and making the best of situations. There is a passivity that leaves an Acadian American with few options other than seeking the advice and help of community members in what to do.

A reflexive question was posed to the members of how it would be different to confront someone that you felt was not being honest with you:

JOSEPH: I can do that, but who wants to do it? People that can't tell the truth are not worth my time[

MARIE: [Who needs them? I live my life, I am honest and if they are going to rip you off I just stay away from them. You can get into an argument with them but where does it lead you. Believe me I have done it (laughs).

CLAIRE: I have seen you do it at work. It seems like it got you nowhere but more aggravation and a headache.

MARIE: That's about it.

JOSEPH: Seriously, I have to do it sometimes, but it never feels good. I have learned to offer a smile and try to get off on the right foot. Someone doesn't respond to that, forget them.

It may be said that this is a typical response by most people in American culture; however, when enactment like this is coupled with the ways of managing interpersonal relationships as noted above, the actions follow moral orders and logical forces that govern a certain way of acting for Acadian Americans. It is not that the Acadian Americans avoid interactions with others out of fear or discomfort; they have created a way of acting that has strong prefigurative forces that tell them how an episode of interaction with people should go. Many experiences with people outside their community, who do not share a similar system of beliefs and forces, have resulted in annoyance and frustrations. Confrontation with others is blocked and prohibited, which leaves few options for a person acting out an Acadian story of relationships with outsiders. Disengaging from others allows the Acadian Americans to manage relationships in a manner that does not threaten the coherence found in Acadian-American stories. Disengagement allows you to work at a level of intensity that is common to members of the community. Avoiding relationships with people who are perceived as not being honest keeps these people outside your community as well. There is little contact with or acknowledgment of these individuals. While the aspects of family, culture, work, and church are permeable, the actions of managing interpersonal relationship with outsiders are not. Interaction with non-Acadians differs from interaction within your own community. The pattern is to adopt a reticent position with non-Acadians, and engage in a different kind of exchange from the communication among members of your community. Interaction within the community is ideally the action of a motivated person, which is a person who coordinates and directs without being overbearing, and ensures that all tasks are accomplished. Interactions with the outside world are conciliatory, reticent, and detached from responsibility of managing people that may annoy you.

Chapter 9

Stories of Vacation and Leisure

WITHIN THE INTERVIEWS there were questions that attempted to explore what vacation and leisure time activities were like among Acadian Americans, and also to learn whether expectations were different for work around the house from those for work at a job. The members shared numerous stories about vacation and leisure time activities, and there seem to be inconsistencies in the stories about vacation and leisure time which will be presented below. In this first transcript two professional males are talking about vacation and leisure time.

INTERVIEWER: *Can you tell me what your vacations are like?*

PAUL: Vacation doesn't matter where I am. Wherever I go people know me. <u>I am on stage all the time. I am always being observed</u> So any time I can go away is good.

INTERVIEWER: *How are vacations different from work?*

PAUL: I am constantly thinking about what's going on back home. If something is going on here, I can't relax. When I am on vacation I will check out other businesses like mine to see what they are doing.

RENE: I enjoy working around the house. I work on the cars, and last summer I built a deck. At home you really get to do it for yourself. Come to think of it that doesn't really sound like relaxing to most people (laughs), but I am happy.

PAUL: Oh God! I am so anal-retentive. My old college roommates say they always invite me just because if we rent a house at a ski mountain or the beach I keep it in great shape. We can be watching TV or talking and I get up to pick up a speck of dust across the room. I make sure we leave the place better than when we got there.

INTERVIEWER: *How is that different from other people you may know?*

PAUL: A lot! (laughs aloud) It's my French heritage coming out. It has to be perfect.

INTERVIEWER: *Who would be most concerned if it was not perfect?*

PAUL: I don't know. Umm . . . I guess I would. I kind of put this pressure on myself, but I am not happy, and I can't relax if things are not just so.

While these members are able to distinguish vacation time as different from work, their actions remain similar when on vacation. One member (Paul) seems to have more difficulty in being away from his job, but then he is a part owner of a business. Rene talks about vacation as working around his house or on his cars, and then quickly follows it with a statement to show that he realizes this is not how vacation is viewed from the outside. Paul talks of the difficulty of relaxing, and goes on to say he cannot relax unless all things are taken care. Things being taken care of must be consistent with his understanding of how things should be. The world must have a certain order that comes about through working, and he has come to realize this through the forces in FCWc.

There is evidence of the Laughing Game being played in this part of the transcript. Paul plays the Laughing Game and acknowledges that his way of acting is different, but then moves to say it's his heritage. He identifies being Acadian as the force that makes him act differently, and being Acadian reaffirms his action because he belongs to a community where this is expected and makes sense to the members there. While there is a communion with the Acadian-American community in stating that it is my heritage, Paul's desire to make things just so, or Rene's working hard at tasks around the house, are the result of prefigurative forces that lead them to act in this way and allow them to act as a good person should act.

In the nonprofessional group, and the other professional group, vacations were described as fun, and at times as total relaxation; yet there were many stories about a feeling of tension while on vacation, much like those described above. People spoke of making lists, and worrying about what they had to do when they returned. In one of the professional groups a member described getting ready for vacation, and how she acted when on vacation in this way:

THERESA: I can't go on vacation unless my laundry is done, everything is put away and the house is clean. My husband laughs at me saying you are not going to be here for the next 10 to 12 days, who is going to see it? I don't care, I have to have it done right. I have actually found that getting ready for vacation, and vacations itself are exhausting.

INTERVIEWER: *What makes vacation exhausting?*

THERESA: I have to work harder to get ready, and then while I am on vacation. I want to make sure everything is right. Meals, for one, if we rent a place where

I can cook. . . . Did I pack enough clothes, or are we going enough places and seeing all that we can? I should tell you all this story about me and vacations. My husband was asked to join this club and part of the membership is that you get complete use of a cabin on the lake right over the border in New Hampshire one weekend a year. The cabin is very rustic, VERY! The club has been around for about seventy-five years. I don't think the cabin was cleaned more than a few times over all those years. One day when my husband took the kids fishing, and I decided to give the place a good scrubbing. When I got done, it looked so much better. After the weekend my husband saw the club president and he stated that my cleaning, and my decorating, just a little bit of decorating (laughs)—I just put a tablecloth on the table, and found some old vases that I put some flowers in, maybe a few other things—but anyway it caused a lot of concern for the other members. See they wanted a rustic cabin, and not a house. They very politely said that if we were to do that again they couldn't let us have the cabin anymore!

INTERVIEWER: *What did you think of their statement?*

THERESA: Well I guess I didn't like it. Why would anyone want to live in filth when things could be so much nicer? The place was a mess cabin or not, and I was making it right. There are kids that come there and eat and sleep. It shouldn't be that dirty.

DORIS: Hmm, if it was me, I would tell them they could keep their cabin. It would drive me crazy to think I would have to live in a mess like that and relax.

For Theresa vacation carries a high degree of obligation to prepare, and then to work at the parenting-work obligations. Theresa was living an Acadian story of what a parent must do for her family, and she was informed of what was right by forces found in FCWc. A vacation does not release Theresa from logical forces that inform her how a good person must act.

The story of the cabin demonstrates the conflict between the meaning system that the Acadian Americans live with in terms of what is expected and must be done, and a world that does not live with similar logical forces. She tells this story in a good-humored way, recognizing that her way of acting is different from other peoples' ways. She found it difficult to imagine a world where it could be any other way, but respects what people there want even though she doesn't agree with it. When Theresa states that the cabin should not be that dirty, she speaks from the Acadian-American view of what a cabin or a place people live in should be like. A rustic dwelling did not represent comfort or relaxation for her. Rustic, or in her view unclean, represents a failure to make things as they should be. The reaction from Doris also serves to reaffirm Theresa's actions and views about how to live. As seen with Paul, relaxing seems difficult for Acadian Americans when things are out or order. The feeling that comes from things being in order is a feeling of satisfaction that fulfills a sense of selfhood, while things out of order creates a different feeling that compels people to work to change this. Relaxing does not mean abandoning the logical forces that drive an Acadian American to work and seek the feeling of fulfillment that work and an orderly world bring.

Theresa's story has a comical tone that she and the other members recognize and respond to with a sense of amusement. Like other patterns of the Laughing Game they see how eccentric their behavior must seem to others, but the moral forces are too strong to abandon the action. Laughing not only affirms their difference from others, but it allows the Acadian Americans to express their own similarities. Other members in the nonprofessional group had similar stories with a comical tone about vacation and the drive that keeps them working even when others expect not to work.

JOSEPH: Vacation isn't rest. Jesus I have to tell you this one. My wife makes draperies, and she did a job for this woman. The woman was so happy with how things came out. She gave us her house at the Cape to use for a weekend. We gets there and my wife says, "Jesus those curtains aren't right. They are driving me crazy." So she takes 'em down and re-hems them, sews them or something . . . took her all day long. But I am just as bad. While she is working on that, there is this front door on the porch that is driving me crazy. It's all crooked, slams funny when it closes. It wasn't hung right. I got my tools in the truck so I say what the hell. I take the door down, and rehang it. It actually cost me about forty bucks for new hardware but the friggin' thing worked right after that though.

ALL: (Laughter)

INTERVIEWER: *What told you to fix the door and not sit on the porch, or go down to the beach?*

JOSEPH: I don't know, it just wasn't right, the door was messed up, and I couldn't enjoy myself knowing that.

MARIE: I know what you mean. My husband and I drove down to Florida to see some friends of ours. When they went to work we sat around by their pool. I keep looking up at this God damn Spanish moss hanging all over her trees. We found some rakes, a ladder, and even a saw and we took the Spanish moss down and trimmed the trees. We worked like dogs. Must have been 98 degrees that day. When she got home, she wasn't so happy though, she kind of liked the Spanish moss.

CLAIRE: (Laughing) Oh Jesus Marie! Yeah, yeah, I know what you mean. Yeah, but we always rent our cottage in Maine to Frenchmen we know around town and they are always doing some kind of repair for us. Pete R, you all know him, the plumber.

JOSEPH: Sure. Good guy.

CLAIRE: Last summer he rented our place and when he got back to town to drop the key off he said I hope you don't mind, but your shower and kitchen sink were driving me nuts so I fixed them. We went up about a week later and when we saw, he replaced the kitchen sink faucet and put a spray hose in, and he put a new showerhead on too. We called him up and told him we were refunding part of the rental, but he said forget it. Those were pieces I had with me and I was bored. It helped me to pass the time.

The stories are related in a joking good-humored way. Other members laugh and extend the stories by telling of a time they did a similar thing. This has reflexive features of continuing the stories, but also serves as recognition of membership in a group of people who act in certain ways that differ from most other people. Extending the stories shows the conjoint process of constructing the stories, and the understanding the members share about working at this level of intensity. The members were asked if they would want to change that and take a vacation where they didn't work. Here is one response:

LINDA: I said to my husband I am going to try to relax this vacation. We went to Montreal for a few days. I woke up the first morning and started to make the bed, he said to me I thought you were going to relax. I stopped. Then the housekeeper came in. She was working really hard and said she had all the rooms to do today because the other girl called in sick. I got on one end of the bed and said, "Come on let me help you. We'll get this room done fast." I gave up. Every morning I made my own bed, collected the towels, and emptied the trash. I felt better, and it only took a minute . . . and the poor girl, she had one less room to do. So no, I am happier working than sitting around like Jackie Onassis.

In this episode the force to work, and to make a difference for a housekeeper, influences the behavior to work instead of relaxing. Working is a coherent action and makes more sense for Linda than sitting around and relaxing. When referring to relaxing Linda and the other members are calling on an understanding of relaxing as rest or time spent doing anything that is not work. It does not make sense to Linda or the others to spend time on a vacation sitting idly. Work is action through which they live their lives, and many things in living a life require work. They are not referring to work as what is found in a job; they are referring to the work of taking care of oneself, family members, and others around you.

At a colloquium at the French Institute at Assumption College in Worcester, Massachusetts (Chetro-Szivos, 2000), I presented material on my research on Acadian Americans and the meaning of working. An audience member offered a comment on these stories about vacation and leisure and added that he had heard Franco-Americans referring to extended time periods off from work that might have been the result of illness, layoffs, or extended vacations referred to as "loafing." He stated that loafing was talked about in the usual negative sense, as something not right. Based on his account, the grammar of loafing has a moral theme. The person who refers to time spent not working as loafing is doing so in a pejorative way. Having the time for loafing removes the person from doing what a person should do, and must do as part of FCWc. The loss of a job in many cases, layoffs, plant closings, accident or injury is not the fault of the person. Yet being out of work causes a level of discomfort (even when benefits are being paid to the person so that failing to provide is less an issue). A term such as *loafing* has an emotional connotation that is especially disagreeable to many Franco-Americans. This feature, consistent across this group of people, shows that the emotional experience of work, or in this case not working, informs people about when they are living a life as it should be lived. Being out of work renders a person unproductive and outside of the forces of what a person should be doing. The emotional component of loafing, not working for any reason at all, is widely felt by members of the population. There are components of the grammar of working, or living a life as a productive person, that are made present through this experience of loafing. The discomfort of loafing or non-productivity indicates the forces that compel Acadians to live their life in a certain manner. Loafing presents an awkward moment in living. As Cronen commented, without certain experiences we are not talking about a life worth living (Cronen, 1995b). These emotional experiences are significant as they mirror Acadian stories about living a life and the relationships that are present in FCWc. In this concept of loafing we can see another facet of the grammar of working. Acadian stories of living are stories of working hard, and being a productive person. Loafing is not what a person does in living a life. The aesthetic produced by loafing has disagreeable features that inform members that things are not going as they should.

This is not to say that vacation and leisure time are considered as loafing, or that vacations are not allowed by the logical forces that inform the behavior of Acadian Americans. Stories of vacation turn into stories of work and being productive. Working is a part of experience of living a good life. Vacations must be lived effectively, and a person should not become idle because it is vacation time. The experience of fulfillment is possible when an Acadian American can satisfy the strong moral forces of obligation, and living in a world where things are "right." The reality of what is right has its own set of rules and definitions that differ from most other peoples' rules and definitions.

Contradictions, Equivocations, and Answers

While there are stories of vacations as a time that members look forward to, there are some apparent contradictions from an outsider's point of view. Here in this section of transcript Doris talks of what she does on vacation.

DORIS: I have a hard time on vacations relaxing because I think of all the things I could be doing. Seriously, I have a hard time. I think of what I have to do when I get home. I think I have this and this—I make lists when I am on vacation for what I am going to do when I get home. But when I am on vacation, I get to run every morning and read novels that I never have time for at home; it's total relaxation. I don't do a thing. Then I have a chance when my husband and I are sitting on the beach to write a post card to each new student I will have in September, adjust my lesson plans, and he does the same thing.

INTERVIEWER: *It seems like you said very different things just now. You said you have a hard time relaxing and you think of what you have to do when you get home, but you do get to relax. Yet when you are relaxing you are working on writing cards to the new children[*

DORIS: [Well I do relax when I read . . . and writing to the children is fun, and then later I won't have to worry about lesson plans. When I say I have a hard time relaxing I mean that I have to work at it. (Laughs) That really sounds funny.

JOAN: (Laughing) Me too! My idea of relaxing on vacation is to buy frozen vegetables instead of making fresh ones, or even going out to eat instead of cooking. God we are pitiful. WHY? (looks at interviewer) Why are we like this? (Laughing) You have got to tell us. Are we sick? (laughs). I want you to, or somebody to tell me why I am like this.

INTERVIEWER: *What do you think?*

JOAN: It's just . . . just . . . that everything has got to be right. Just so. Perfect, our mothers and fathers did it, we do it, our kids will do it. God forbid that they won't. Work, work, work, work, WORK! I guess it's better than being on welfare or having a drinking problem (laughs). Hey I feel good when things are OK, so what if you have to work to make it that way. It's worth it.

ALL: (Laughing)

The apparent contradictions are found in statements such as Doris's, where she talks about having a hard time relaxing because she is thinking of all the things that must be done when she returns home. This is much like Theresa's report earlier about having to work hard before going on vacation, then working hard while on vacation to make sure all things are going well. These actions fit the description of what a motivated person must do, as discussed earlier in the interviews: A motivated person must assume responsibility and follow through on all tasks, as well as anticipate the future and what will need to be done. These directions tell a motivated person how to act and how to work.

Initially Doris's statements sound like contradictions, but she is working at vacation and making sure that issues for her family, job, and the larger community are attended to. This is how an Acadian story of living a life must go. Vacation offers a break from the everyday routine of home life and what is present in that context, but it does not mean that Doris or any of these members may stop meeting the forces of their lives, which are to work. For Doris, it is the work of making lists, fulfilling amounts of time in reading, running, and preparing for the school year ahead. Doris offers the idea that she must work at vacation, which is what a good person does. Working at something may be the only way to ensure that it is done correctly—including relaxing or recreation.

Joan's question to the interviewer indicates the difference that may be felt by the members between the world they live within and the world they see around them. Joan and the others recognize, as indicated by the laughter and comments about how funny this must sound, that there are people living their lives differently. They call upon the Laughing Game to reaffirm their actions. Joan directs a question to the interviewer about whether that are "sick", which seems to seek an affirmation from an outsider about how they live. However, when Joan is asked a question reflecting her question, she offers information about logical forces in FCWc. She first talks of a shared rule that has been raised by many of the other members and that is that everything has to be "so." Things that are "so" are not out of order or in conflict with the rules that inform the members of what order is. There is a shared knowledge about when things are in order and "just so" at home, in your community and at work. The link to family and culture is present as she states, "we saw our mothers and fathers do it." Joan and the others saw actions of their parents and the meanings of these actions were understood in terms of lived practice. The logical forces appear to offer her a satisfactory answer to her own question. The conversants are able to act with one another because they share notions as to what they will do next. These expectations are familiar to them because of the interactions that have made up their experience of living as an Acadian American. Warriner (1970) stressed that a shared perspective is necessary for ongoing communication that is central to cooperation and common understanding of how to act. For Joan and these members, making sense is not limited to seeing their parents' action or hearing that things must be so. Making sense is present in their ability to extend or develop action in a coherent way. These rules for living in a world where things are so are not private themes. As the other members talk about this theme it is evident that it is a socially shared rule.

Joan talks about how Acadians are people who work to make the world perfect as her parents had done, she does, and she imagines "our kids will." The use of the word "our" indicates a sense of community as she speaks for all Acadian Americans and their children. Joan also expresses fear that their children may not act as her generation which followed the generation before. She expresses a wish that "God forbid" the kids will not act like them in the future. Joan and many of the members recognize Acadian-American stories are threatened from the outside which has different stories of how to live a life. This threat is felt when episodes of living, or working, are seen as different, or even eccentric by others.

Joan goes on to say that the way Acadian Americans act is better than being on welfare or having a drinking problem. As we have seen, the idea of being on public assistance violates many of the beliefs of Acadian Americans.[1] Public assistance compromises a sense of independence, pride, and doing it for yourself. It also means that you are loafing and not being productive and contributing to your family, or community, or living as a good person does. Relying on public assistance violates a moral order of how to live a life. What tells her that this is a better way to live is that she feels good when things are OK or just so. Working to achieve this feeling is worth it to her even if it is odd compared to other people's standards.

What may be seen as contradictions to an outsider are not contradictions to the Acadian American. An outsider is likely to see work and relaxation as opposing ideas, but the Acadian American does not. There is work an Acadian American does when on vacation that is "relaxing work" as opposed to "job work." Within their meaning system working at vacation, doing the things that must be done, has a logic and is coherent to the members of this group.

Working at Hobbies

Another aspect of working is working at hobbies or tasks around the home that are thought to be enjoyable, such as gardening. Questions were asked to determine how this kind of work differed from working for your family, at a job, or when you were on vacation. Members seem to experience the same forces and work as intently as they do at other times. This section of transcript shows what that kind of work is like.

INTERVIEWER: *Is there a difference between kinds of work at home and at your job? For example, let's say you have a flower garden in your yard, do you work differently at that than you do at your job?*

CLAIRE: No, not at all

MARIE: No

CLAIRE: One's a hobby but you still work at it as best you[

MARIE: [It's important to me to do it right.

JOSEPH: Can't be any weeds in that garden[

CHARLIE: [EXACTLY

MARIE: (laughs) Its got to be clean[

CLAIRE: [It has to be nice, you can't go around doing things half-assed or you won't feel good, you will feel guilty. If there are weeds it's not being done right, then you got to bed and think Oh my God I have to get out there tomorrow and fix it, it's not right.

MARIE: I know gardening is supposed to be fun, but if I go to my daughter's game I am thinking oh my God, what am I doing? I have to get my flowers, or water them. It can feel awful if you aren't doing it right.

JOSEPH: My wife already bought my sunflower seeds yesterday. I am all set.

CLAIRE: Sometimes we make things a little stressful, especially in the spring or summer until you get everything in the yard the way you want it.

INTERVIEWER: *What are the times you feel most relaxed like, can you describe them?*

MARIE: My relaxation time is right before bed. I make sure I read at least every night.

JOSEPH: Early morning wake-ups for me. I wake up at quarter to five and I sit in a chair and think of what I need to do in the day. No TV, no music, no nothing. The older I get, the quieter I like it.

MARIE: It doesn't get much better than times when everybody is sleeping and it's just me. I have a cup of coffee, get the wash going, read the paper, you know, just things.

CLAIRE: I love it like that too.

JOSEPH: That's a vacation to be able to do something you don't have to do.

MARIE: But to get back to working in the garden, that's a vacation too. You make something look good. You take your time, and the place looks nice

The members describe the intensity of working at hobbies as the same for them as it would be at a job, or taking care of their families. Even with a hobby, they feel they must do the best job that they can do and not doing the best possible job can leave them with feelings of guilt. Claire describes gardening as an activity that is supposed to be fun, but can result in feeling awful if it is not done right. The enjoyment in such an activity is found in the good feeling it produces when it is done right, but guilt and the obligation to do the job well also acts as a force on their actions. Claire recognizes that they can make their lives stressful by wanting to get a garden to look a certain way, but the satisfaction and feeling that can come from working at it are worth working hard for.

The deontic operator of obligation is experienced when working at a hobby or a task that is thought of as pleasurable. Members feel an obligation to do the job the right way, which has implications for working hard at a task. Members know when things are done in the right way, by looking at the result, and the sense of satisfaction they feel. Within work that is pleasurable work, or a hobby, there are the same strong prefigurative forces the members feel at a job, or working for their family.

PART THREE

Work, Communication, and Selfhood

Chapter 10

Making Sense of the Acadian-American Stories

THE STORIES THE ACADIAN-AMERICAN MEMBERS SHARED about working, family life, church, motivated people, and vacation and leisure time provided situated encounters of people living in episodes of interaction and conversations. Pearce (1989) described these interactions as taking place in a "recurring and reflexive process where resources are expressed in practices and in which practices (re)construct resources" (page 23). It is within these conversations that the behavior of the Acadian Americans can be understood by recognizing the meanings that inform their interactions. The communication people shared in the interviews was critical to understanding what working means to them and how they live their lives. The stories provided answers to the research questions posed earlier in this work. The interviews contained stories about working hard, what it means to work hard, and how working contributes to living a life. CMM regards the stories people tell and the stories they live as important aspects of understanding their lives. The stories here are not seen as simple accounts of the lives of Acadian Americans. They reveal and organize the social practices and beliefs of this group. Each group has its stories of how to act as a successful member of that group, and members must be enmeshed in those stories and act according to the practices of the group. While there are no universal stories about living a life, there are a number of stories here that people generally called upon. These stories showed how they live in the world and are active participants in creating its structure. The study demonstrated that these people living in action constructed their own stories, which made up their social realities. The content of the stories provided information that was consistent and meaningful within this community. The stories of Acadian Americans, like those of all people, are held together in a nonlinear hierarchy. The hierarchy of stories illustrated a way of working that effects what it is to be a person, and how work is a central aspect of selfhood. The findings do not suggest or attempt to discover a logical order to these stories. Instead, the data indicate that within this culture there are connections among members between the stories, and there are ways the stories fit together in living as an Acadian American. Work is featured prominently in living a life and the data revealed coherent features within these stories about working and how working contributes to living a life to members of this group. Within the data there are some slight variations between professionals and nonprofessionals, and differences between womens and men's work roles, but there are consistent logical forces, and grammars of meaning that run through all of these stories.

Within these stories being an individual is seen as a personal accomplishment, but this is achieved through actions that are extended through social institutions, emotions, coherent social practices, and moral orders that make up Acadian-American culture. What may appear as a conflict between individuality and social life begins to make sense when the analysis reveals the recursive features of action between the individual and the culture. Dewey provided clarity on this issue when he explained that " individuality cannot be opposed to association. It is through association that man has acquired his individuality and it is through association that he exercises it" (1967). For Dewey, individuality did not mean separation from others. He saw selfhood as only possible within the community. The concept of self and community are not opposing positions, and in fact the data here show that selfhood is made possible by a strong and inseparable affiliation with the community. Within the Acadian American community successful enactment is found in how hard you work, and the ways you work. This enactment can be seen by others, and is experienced on a personal level through work. The interviews showed the inextricable links between self, family, culture, religion, and work which are presented in this chapter. These stories were recollections of episodes of working which represent levels of understanding about working. This understanding shapes the meaning of the episodes for the participants. The stories that are shared and recounted reinforce coherent ways of acting to the members of this community. CMM contends that communication and meaning arise in the process of action with others. This analysis looked at these situated encounters of action and episodes that are part of the world of these people, and found that the living and telling of stories served to constitute and reaffirm the actions and grammar of working. Evidence of this was seen in the interactions where people extended stories of another speaker, and showed strong relation to the content of what was being discussed.

Grammars of Working and Identity

The interviews were focused on locating the grammar of working and identity Acadian Americans employed. The interviews also attempted to locate how coherence and coordination of these grammars were achieved in the stories they lived. The use of a term, such as *working*, is dependent on its use in conversation among members of a group. Terms can have different meanings among different groups of people, but the use of a term adheres to a set of rules that are shared by the members of a group, thereby making the term intelligible to them. The grammar of a term includes the rules that help the members to make sense of the meaning of words and the actions associated with them. The rules and grammar serve the important task of informing the members how to act with others and achieve coherence. Calling on Wittgenstein, "a meaning of a word is a kind of employment of it. For it is what we learn when the word is incorporated into our language"(1969). Grammar, in the Wittgensteinian sense, is not limited to words. It is extended to concepts and actions. Therefore, making sense of a word or concept is more than an ability to recognize it. Understanding is the capability to act according to patterns of action that have developed in situated practice. In this study, Acadian-American ideas of working include the feelings, as well as behavior and actions of working in a particular way. It was shown that *working* is much more than a word with a common definition that means the same thing in all cultures. The data show that working has its own grammar to the Acadian Americans, and it is a prominent feature of their conversational interaction, and of their selfhood. Working included themes and actions of honesty, pride, being "motivated", providing for your family, and "doing it for yourself." These themes made up the grammar of working. Knowing the meaning of the term working for Acadian Americans is to know the patterns of specific behavior, feelings, and practices associated with working. Their ideas of working are the result of situated encounters and structure that guides their interaction within their community. The reflexive features of their interaction demonstrated their ability to coordinate their notions of work and achieve a coherence that was mutually intelligible to the members.

Work does not mean the same thing in all places, and by exploring their grammar it was found that Acadian Americans relate to work in different ways from members of most other groups. A striking difference in their grammar of working is that they do not make a distinction between work at home or at a job. The participants discussed the difficulties in distinguishing between what is done at a job or at home. They see little difference in the way a person works at home or at a job. In fact, they spoke of the same forces and obligations influencing them to work "hard" at home, on the job, or in the community. Working hard has a link to all aspects of selfhood and how one is a member of a community.

These understandings and beliefs reveal the grammar of working differs from other people's ideas of what working means. The features of working that are particular to the Acadian Americans allow them to act according to patterns of action that have developed in their situated practices, and thereby achieve coherence.

Moral Orders

The study revealed the moral and logical forces that inform the grammar of working for Acadian Americans. It was found that to be an Acadian American one must work, and work hard at all things. This direction of what a person must do, can do, must not do, and cannot do is evidence of social life being a moral matter. Rules, active in the grammar of working, tell people what is appropriate in a situation, and what consequences are likely to occur. As distinct grammars are developed among the members of a community through the process of communication, selfhood also emerges. However, as Cronen explained moral theory must account for the unity of self and action which are created and sustained in the primary social process (1991). CMM is concerned with rules and how they constitute a moral order and are necessary to achieve coherence in human action. Selfhood is not the same in all cultures, which should tell us that different moral orders exist concurrently with different forms of selfhood. As described by Pearce (1989), a moral order includes a set of practices and resources that promote morality. The stories that Acadian Americans shared in the interviews are replete with moral orders and forces that must be followed. CMM points to deontic operators as present in human action. The deontic operators are divided into actions that the individual consciously enacts (legitimate, undetermined, prohibited, or obligatory) and those that are beyond individual control (caused, blocked, probable, or random). These forces tell people what is logical in terms of meaning and how they should act. This logical force impacts the interpretations people make of situations, and how to respond to events and objects they are confronted with. The analysis explored and identified the moral orders and the impact of these orders on how people view work and act when working. The moral order within the narratives helped to describe what is present in actions and communication. The moral orders for Acadian Americans come from FCWc and have a strong force on their lives as demonstrated in the analysis. The most prominent forces felt by the members were the deontic operators of obligatory and blocked action. As mentioned above obligation is an operator that the individual consciously enacts and this was seen in many of the actions of motivated people who have learned to act as motivated persons or good persons would. The blocking of action is seen as not within the person's control, and this occurred when forces in FCWc prevented the members from an action. These moral forces influenced the meaning and action both within organizations and in all settings. Acadian Americans do not make distinctions between work in any settings; the moral forces remain the same in all places.

There are some differences in moral and logical forces when dealing with the outside world. As indicated in the findings the members recognize that they live in a world of differences from most other people, and as a result, they manage these relationships with others in particular ways. The strong prefigurative forces to work in certain ways inform the Acadian Americans of what must be done. They will act to satisfy these forces and work hard but not in a manner that draws attention. The grammar of a motivated person has clear rules for action in all settings. When working in organizations with diverse populations, Acadian Americans do not complain about others. They do their job and when possible complete the work of others. However when dealing with this outside world at work or in the community, there is a hesitancy. This hesitancy is manifest in decisions not to manage others and to keep business dealings within their community whenever possible.

The consequences of actions in the work setting do not present significant change for the Acadian Americans. They are more likely to live by the deeply-felt forces within their own community. However, the Acadian Americans have found ways to be a part of organizations and make contributions, as evidenced in the number of stories about working that were analyzed.

Aesthetic Dimensions

During the interviews the Acadian Americans make a distinction between working in the right way and not working in the right way. It is not possible to understand the grammar and forces of working without recognizing the aesthetical dimensions of their experience. When the Acadian Americans talk about the right way of working, they feel a strong sense of accomplishment. When they do not work in the right way, they feel a strong sense of guilt. Lived experience includes aesthetic dimensions that are an essential feature of experience. What is felt cannot be overlooked in the process of inquiry because aesthetics reveals aspects of working that are important to understanding the prominence of work for Acadian Americans. The concept of a somatic aesthetic transcends what is simply said and points to the ineffable nature of communication. Exploring the nuances of aesthetics provides more information about the experiences that contribute to the grammar of working and the behavior of working hard. The interviews showed how feelings and actions organized and symbolized their experiences. Locating aesthetics in the depth of lived experience enriches understandings of the grammar of working and provides more description about what meanings are informing behavior. Through the interviews, efforts were made to find where and how Acadian Americans learn to find satisfaction in working hard. The consummatory nature of working is evident in feelings of satisfaction, or guilt. This was recognized as a shared feeling between the members and it provides a heightened sense of identity and membership in a community of people who act and feel a certain way about working. Although aesthetics are produced and felt by individuals, there is a relationship with the aesthetics of working with the community itself. Dewey expressed this idea when he pointed out that aesthetical experiences are produced and enjoyed by individuals, but they become what they are within the context of their experience because of the culture in which they participate (Dewey, 1934). Aesthetics are both an individual and a cultural matter, as we see in this community. Dewey also saw an aesthetic moment as the moment when things come together in a beautiful fit, and it may be unexpressed in words, yet we deeply appreciate it. The aesthetical dimensions are active features of experience. This aesthetic of working is active in many of the stories and episodes discussed in the interviews. The members talked of the feelings both beautiful and awkward when they related stories about working. The content of these stories helps to make sense of the meaning of the term working. By accounting for the aesthetical dimension there is a deeper understanding of the grammar of the term *working*.

Action outside the Workplace

As stated above, how one works and the forces for working remain the same in all places. The interviews addressed the research question about what stories of work extend beyond the consequentiality of action outside the workplace. It was evident that the forces for action remain consistent in all places for the Acadian Americans. The members continue to work hard while on vacation and at hobbies, with some slight differences between vacation and hobbies, and work at job, family life, or in their community. The members describe the differences as a break from daily routines, but they are still working. It may be said that all people work at hobbies, or vacations, but the striking difference for Acadian Americans is the unvarying pace at which they work at all things. There is the same intensity for all tasks in all places.

On several occasions members stated that they needed to *work at* vacation, or *work at* relaxing. Even successful vacation or relaxation can only be achieved through working hard at it. This use of language demonstrates how the members view work as a means to live effectively. Work will bring feelings of satisfaction that may not be found in many other ways. A friend shared a story about her father who is Acadian-American, and who retired a short while ago. She remarked how he works at his retirement activities with the same intensity and verve that he worked at his carpentry job. He lives according to a strict schedule of golf time, yard work, church activities, visiting grandchildren, and keeping himself busy. She states that he often remarks he has so much to do and needs to budget his time better. This is unlike other stories of retirement where people stay busy, but may not feel the forces to get all the activities accomplished or to feel obligations to use the time better.

Acadian Americans derive a great deal of satisfaction from the world being "just so." The story of Joseph sitting on the porch while on vacation and being bothered by the door is not as much a story of work as it is a story of making the world "just so." The Acadian Americans work to keep the world "just so" because it is what a good person must do in all instances, and it fulfills a sense of selfhood. A world that is just so has an aesthetical dimension that reflects a beautiful fit with a life that is lived. Work is not regarded as toil or drudgery, or as something to be avoided. Work is the means to derive selfhood, enjoy the aesthetics of life, and to be a member of a community. This conception of working is different from most other people's idea of work and at times it may seem peculiar to the outside world. The members are aware of this difference, and they talk about this openly in the stories they shared in the interviews. Regardless of these differences, Acadian Americans continue to work hard at all things, including their hobbies and leisure activities. Within this community this is a social reality they have created that has forces for actions that are seen in their situated encounters.

Chapter 11

Conclusions
and the Story of Work

In this study numerous stories of Acadian-American life emerged, and these stories played an important role in exploring the grammar of the term *working* within this culture. The exploration of these stories served as a starting point to answer why working is featured so prominently in the lives of these individuals. Most importantly, communication was shown as a constitutive force that shaped their social life and practices. It is through their communication that they have constructed, maintained, and modified the grammar of working. The stories they told and the stories they lived revealed the forces for action, and why work is a critical feature of living a good life. An Acadian-American story revealed how these people are unique, what makes their way of working unique, and how this cultural view of work contributes to understanding what work is. Developing an understanding of the Acadian-American grammar of working shows the significance of peoples' communication practices.

A Contextual View

The findings do not reveal foundational beliefs about work, or Acadian Americans. As it has been argued by Dewey, foundational conceptions are not available and not needed for human practices (Shusterman, 1997). This is a cultural view of working that sees experience at the core of understanding working. A cultural view may be called a contextual view, as it accounts for the connections shared by the members through a process of experience. Experience is a way of describing the relationships between the individual, society, and institutions. What experience is not is the inner consciousness of the individual. Personal consciousness is a product of experience, it is not the source of experience. It was James (1912) who described experience as a continuum of parts that flow together and form a unity. James and other pragmatists have described experience as a confluence of persons' abilities and the phenomena of the world in situated action (Dewey, 1920/1948; James, 1909; Mead & Morris, 1934). The perspective of a life as a unity of events differs from traditional views which see life as a series of distinctions and separate pieces. The connections among events are without gaps or cleavages and experience accounts for this continuity. Dewey's view of experience includes the action of doing, sensation, idea, and the course for action. He saw the mind as the connection of earlier and later elements in an ongoing and active process. These vibrant features of the quality of experience has a concern with the future. Experience expresses this unity of thought and action as seen in the active adjustments the individual makes to the environment. We put ideas into action using these very ideas as instruments for reconstructing experience and acting into the future. The relationship between the individual and the environment occurs in a recursive manner as the person does something to the environment, and the environment in turn does something to the person. Dewey (1916) expressed this as the dual nature of experience. He regarded experience as the connection or learning that comes about as part of this passive and active relationship between person and environment. Cronen (2000b) stated that experience describes both the means and outcomes of interaction, and he called upon Dewey's notion that communication describes the human process of interaction in which experience is made and used. Experience is more than a psychic event. It is the transaction between the person and their environment which points beyond a person's thinking, feeling, and reactions to events. It includes the process of interaction and the continuous connection between what we think, what we do, and the consequent.

The concerns with experience in this study focus on developing an understanding of the unity of the Acadian Americans' experience, and the means and outcomes of interactions in which experience is made and used. Accounting for their experience will help to understand the association of ideas with what is present in the contexts they live within, and to make sense of the actions they use that form an Acadian–American grammar of working. Experience connects the Acadian Americans to the world. The experience of working is organized in a continuity of elements which proceed from the patterns of practices the Acadian Americans participate in. When referring to the word work there are particular activities woven into its meaning, and the meaning of working entails a series of actions based upon the Acadian Americans' unity of experience.

This contextual view, relying on experience, sees the members participating in an integrative process of thoughts and action which is made in association with the logical forces of family, culture, working, and church. A contextual view recognizes that thoughts and practices are drawn from the environment and the experiences that compose a life. A contextual view is a way of looking at how objects and episodes (which do not exist in isolation, but by connection) form complex patterns. This view is in line with an evolutionary point of view that Cronen (2000b) described as a perspective that observes the way one event enters into the nature of the next and how that opens and closes possibilities for the future. An evolutionary view does not seek cause-and-effect relationships that move toward a predetermined end. The world is not seen as stationary or at rest, and this certainly includes communication that is regarded as extending into the future. The ongoing process of interaction leads in multiple directions that are not predictable, or reducible to universal concepts. This view seeks to make sense of the way people living in interaction form the basis of coherent thought and action, and it is always mindful of how their processes move toward the future. This view is significant in understanding the Acadian Americans' relationship to working. Understanding working does not mean that we analyze it as an object that is at rest. Making sense of the Acadian Americans' grammar of working includes an exploration of how people act, feel, and form coherent practices that are part of the experience of working. The Acadian Americans make use of the past, make sense of the present, and act into the future. In so doing they create the world they live within, where working serves as a way of living a life.

Directions of the Research

This study concerned itself with exploring the grammar of working among Acadian Americans, emphasizing the influence of context on the action of the members. This perspective guides the researcher to directly observe actual episodes of behavior. Removing the communication from its natural context would make the data suspect (Leeds-Hurwitz, 1995). As a result of the researcher entering into the interaction and thus the grammar, data emerged that revealed the structure of rules and practices that the members used. The method had to allow the researcher to join in the grammar of the participants, while remaining flexible and open to the infinite possibilities for action that existed in the creation and interaction of social practices that made up social reality. In addition, the method must recognize the temporal and kinetic attributes of communication, and that it occurs in situated practice and interaction. This research took account of the feelings, surroundings, and rhythm of members' communication and interactions. A position that includes these dimensions allowed the study to be unbounded by mechanical or holistic conceptions, and thus cultivated what James (1909) and Geertz (1973) have called a thick description. A thick description of the Acadian American's meaning of working will show it is an intricate mesh of feelings, utterances, and actions, and it is a unique take on what working means.

CMM has been characterized as a practical theory because of an ability to offer a way to join in with the grammars of people and thus explore their patterns of action. More than this, CMM assists the researcher in developing percepts to coordinate findings for analysis (Cronen, 1991; Cronen, 2000b; Cronen & Chetro-Szivos, 2001). This gradual process of coming to know does not proceed in private, or as a function of individual consciousness. It transpires by enabling the researcher to enter into the practices and grammar of the group of study. This follows a process much like Peirce described where meaningfulness comes about by gravitating toward knowing, but this knowing is not a private matter. Trial and error are replaced within a communication of common sense and science (Peirce, 1905). By entering into the grammar of the group under study, in time the researcher will come to distinguish the stories present in the conversations. Through this active engagement with the group, the researcher comes to know how the interactions are held together by coherence and accord shared by members of this community. Inquiry that recognizes that interactions are held together by consonance and coherence breaks from methods that seek to discover stationary and hidden mechanisms of behavior. Discovering the hidden objects and essences of people has been a goal of positivist approaches to social research. Within this tradition it is believed that people and their minds could be objectively known. The research usually focuses on identifying those elements that constitute the mind as a stable and fixed object. These methods have proven to be effective in certain contexts, but they are not able to fully account for the active and transient features of communication and conjoint action. CMM, in the tradition of American pragmatism, regards selfhood and thinking as created in the ongoing course of communication. Therefore CMM views situated action as an active process, and the means by which people create and share their own particularized construction of the social world. The goal of CMM is not to discover certitude and primary substances. It is concerned with how people conjointly create patterns of practice that make up their forms of life (Cronen, 1995b).

In enacting Acadian-American stories, people connect antecedent activity with consequent results. CMM recognizes this contextual view and explores the elements of antecedent, act, and consequent. CMM formalized these three elements as a forming coordination in which past, present, and future intersects in the unity of experience. The episodes the participants related demonstrated this forming coordination. What was apparent in these interviews is that the members knew how to act into the community they shared which had expectancy and requirements for action. The members had an ability to see a situation in its continuity from a prior state to eventual outcomes, and made coherent outcomes explicit through their actions.

The Importance of the Stories

Recognizing the depth of FCWc and the inseparable nature of these elements is vital to understand the importance of stories lived and told about the grammar of working, the logical and moral forces for working, and the consequentiality of communication. As demonstrated numerous times, it is not possible for an Acadian American to talk of any one of these elements without talking about the others. Work therefore is deeply embedded and entwined with notions of family, culture, and church. The story of work for Acadian Americans is a story of family, community, and religious belief. The Acadian Americans provide an extraordinary example because their construction of work shows us that work is not inflexible, nor does it mean the same thing in all places. They also show that approaching working as what people do in lived action, as opposed to an object, provides new understandings about work. Working has a shared meaning to the Acadian Americans because of the grammatical abilities that are brought to bear on their communication practices. The forces in FCWc are reinforced through numerous interactions, and in these interactions there are rules and practices that make up the structure of their world. The structure of the Acadian-American life has within it resources that have an intimacy beginning with family, shared with their culture, present within their work, and found within their religious beliefs. This intimacy keeps them different from others, and it reaffirms a sense of selfhood and ways of acting in the world. Living as a member of this culture means that you need to reaffirm the rules and practices found here. The weaving together of the rules, forces, and practices are so firm that it almost makes it impermeable at times. Yet it has flexibility that allows a good person to act with others who may be outside of your culture, to make a difference. In so doing you, your family, your culture, and your religion are reaffirmed. Due to the depth of the experience of work, working means something very different for Acadian Americans than it would for other people in other places.

The rules the Acadian Americans used to guide their action within FCWc were created and sustained by their community. They adapted to challenges in a way that satisfied the rules and forces in FCWc and remained coherent for them. When Acadian Americans are faced with challenges, they make choices based upon their interaction with the environment they live within. Stories such as those related about mothers who must live by principles of doing all you can do in spite of difficulties and tensions, or motivated people who have to manage relations with people who conceptualize work differently are examples of the challenges that may be unique to contemporary life. A course of action may require new adaptations that are based on these commonly shared beliefs about what a good person can and cannot do.

The grammar of working serves an important function, as members will call upon the rules and practices that guide their action within episodes of working. Grammars emerge out of and in peoples' experiences. Stories lived and told about working are embedded in honesty, pride, motivation, and doing it for yourself. Members know what working means and how to enact stories of working according to the rules found in FCWc. The general story of working is a story of how one lives as a good person. The members that were interviewed in this study had developed a shared grammar that indicated a level of understanding and shared practices associated with working, at home, at a job, and in all places. This grammatical ability directed their action in a manner that allowed them to satisfy rules and forces as well as achieve coherence in their interactions.

Practice in Communication Patterns

The CMM analysis of the interviews revealed that the Acadian Americans made use of a communication pattern to address conflicts and tensions within episodes of interaction. This communication practice illustrates the nature of communication that the members used to construct their understanding of working and other integral aspects of their lives. On many occasions during the interviews, the participants would respond to a question by the interviewer, or to a comment by another participant in the group. The pattern would begin when members would recognize a conflict or tension existed in a story of living, or was present in the immediate interaction. The pattern was initiated when the members in the conversation would examine an event, or what was said in the interaction. This initiation of the pattern would serve as a punctuation point as the flow of the conversation, and often its intensity, would change. The group would work together to resolve the issue, or to transform it into an Acadian-American story of how to address this event. Acknowledgment of the problem was offered by other conversants by telling a story where similar things happened to them or someone they knew. Usually the members participated through a process of interposing a number of like stories for a period of time. A variant was evident when the members would speak from a third person position about how the tension should be addressed. The members were aware that something was occurring that required their reflection, and as noted in the preceding chapter, their participation was vigorous, with members offering comments or nonverbal cues to the group. The piling-on of stories would continue until the final punctuation point was achieved. The termination was understood by the members and evident when they reached a sense of agreement. Understanding included aesthetical dimensions evident in their vocal and physical expressions.[1]

Ends-in-View

The piling-on of stories and comments has similar features to what Dewey described as the ends-in-view. The end-in-view serves to guide action to the terminal punctuation point in the interaction. The end-in-view is not the out-

come, although the actual outcome can be identical, but the end-in-view operates differently from the outcome itself. The end-in-view may be thought of as
a projection that works as the instrument to accomplish the actual end or consequences. It is important that people call upon an end-in-view that will bring
about some desired or acceptable ends. Acadian-American notions desired or
acceptable ends are found within the community itself or the logical forces
found in FCWc. Acadian Americans have placed high value on ideas of honesty,
motivation, making a difference, and doing it for yourself. In fact these ideas
appear to have an object status as ends in themselves. However, an interpretation from a pragmatic position would treat these concepts not as what is
acceptable or desired, but as forces for how the acceptable or desired ends can
be attained in the present situation. These are not things, they are means connected to past experiences that direct the members how to act into this
moment. Enacting an episode of honesty or motivation leads action to the
desired or acceptable end. Honesty and motivation are guides to what a good
person does. The Acadian-American grammar of honesty and motivation are
what Dewey referred to as modifiers for action. Dewey would see these as
"tools of insight" that prompt a person to respond to situations (1920/1948).
He thought people resolve challenges by projecting ends-in-view that weigh
the existing conditions in the present difficulties, the desired resolution of the
issue, and the likely consequences for action. The end-in-view serves as the plan
to arrange possibilities for action into a process that brings about the desired or
acceptable state. However, ends-in-view must meet moral standards of what can
or cannot be done and meet the criteria of efficiency and efficacy. Efficiency
and efficacy are highlighted here because in many of the situations that the
Acadian Americans were confronted with, they chose a course of action among
an array of alternatives. Their choices are based upon what actions satisfy the
rules and forces in their lives, and allows them to meet their desired ends. Efficiency and efficacy provides an interpretation of why Acadian Americans, who
act as motivated persons, avoid management positions. As stated earlier, an Acadian-American story of a motivated manager would be a manager that must
complete the work of all the people under their supervision. Efficiency and
efficacy indicates it is better to avoid these difficult management positions
because not everyone that you would manage would have the same relationship
to working. Assuming the role of a manager is not efficient in light of the things
a manager would be required to do. Serving as a manager or leader in your
community is possible because you are responsible for people who share the
same grammatical abilities, but it is not efficient when dealing with people who
have a different story about working.

    Desired or acceptable ends are produced through the process of conjoint
action between the members and it forms the structure of FCWc. In the situated
encounters presented in the study, members are actively judging, or weighing

out choices prior to action. The members grapple with the best course of action in a situation—the one that satisfies the expectations of an Acadian-American story. Over time, success in one situation may play the part of an end-in-view in a future situation and evolve into a value (Gouinlock, 1972). Yet even the applicability of a value is not clear in each situation and the members enter into the pattern to determine or affirm how to enact stories guided by their values. The process is manifest in their interaction. The most appropriate course of action is often not readily apparent, and their communication becomes a process of inquiry in which they search for the best course of action in a communal fashion. Dewey's account of inquiry sees the person as identifying elements of imbalance or discord. That part of experience judged to be involved in the discord is called a "determinate situation." The inquirer's task is to predicate judgment about the situation, and this judgment implicates decisive lines of action that have consequences that can be assessed (Dewey, 1938). The inquirer makes judgments that "warrants the assertion" of those judgments, and in so doing ways of acting are selected in light of the projected consequences. The person or persons are involved in making adjustments to the environment. It is here that people and phenomena intersect (Cronen & Chetro-Szivos, 2001). Inquiry brings order and coherence to situations that are incongruous and conflicted. Dewey saw inquiry as having a communal function to it, and he placed a premium on socially shared experience. Dewey thought it was in inquiry that people achieve communion (Thayer, 1968). He saw coherent experience as communicative and communal, and inquiry as a source of human growth. This coherent experience, and its communal aspects, were evident in the sections of the transcripts that were presented earlier.

The communication process that the Acadian Americans employ is integral in determining a coherent course of action, and satisfies the rules found within the structure that guides their practices and community. The process also shows the constitutive and recursive features of communication that has people and structure intertwined in an evolving and fluid course.

Communion as Coherence

As indicated earlier in the study, the Acadian Americans participate in a communication practice that resembles the sacrament of communion. This shared experience is an active exchange with features of true conjoint action. It is through this communication practice that social knowledge is created and the co-construction of experience goes on. Through this communion process, the group adapts to new situations they encounter, make adjustments to the environment they interact with, and reaffirm the forces in FCWc to maintain coherence. The Acadian Americans process these situations publicly, and thus find a better way to address common issues and reaffirm their community.[2]

An evolutionary view tells us that reality is not fixed. We are always in the process of inquiry and adaptation. The Acadian Americans call upon the process of communion to create knowledge, adapt knowledge, reaffirm their sense of self, and reaffirm the meaning of working. This process is the means that people use to adapt and make sense of the world they live within. They create and reaffirm ways of acting to attain certain purposes and make effective adaptations to the environment.

Within this communication practice we can see how communication itself is constitutive and the primary social process that results in how the Acadian Americans live. What serves as social reality is brought about by an active interpretation of events. However, the action does not come to rest within this communal process of making sense of events. A course of action may be developed and reaffirmed among the members, but it is not a well-finished idea. The action is continuous and the Acadian Americans use their grammatical abilities to retell stories and acknowledge what is going on in the environment, address challenges, and reaffirm their community. This can only be achieved through the process of communication. FCWc provides the rules and practices that the members employ like a map or illustration of what a good person must do. However, it is in this communication process that thought is made public, as the speaker raises the tension to a public level, and the members use grammatical abilities for action and move toward a desired end.

The symbols the Acadian Americans rely on for their communication are imbued with imperfection which leads to multiple possibilities for expression and construction of ways to accomplish coherence. The imperfection of communication, when coupled with the diverse constructions of reality, is evidence that multiple interpretations of the "right way" to address an issue will occur. Cronen (1991) said the eventualities are impossible to project because of the consequentiality of communication; that is, there is no way to predict the course and effects of conjoint, situated action. The members' conjoint action may lead them in numerous directions, and the situations that come before them exist at different points in time which presents different challenges in light of the changing contexts. The challenges they are confronted with today are not the same challenges that their parents faced. There are differences between the worlds they live in now and the world at another point in time, and these differences may signal the need for different courses for action. The course of action must adhere to the socially constructed features of FCWc. However, it's not through these incomplete symbols alone that coherence is attained. Understanding the Acadian Americans' practice is achieved by looking beyond the mere symbols and at their grammar and grammatical abilities. Their grammatical abilities include the capacity to know what a good life is and how working is an indispensable aspect of that life.

Aesthetics, Consummatory Experience, and Punctuation

Throughout the interviews the members talked about the importance of the feelings that tell them when things are right. Members described the feeling that accompanies episodes of "making a difference" or making things "just so." In the episodes of communion, the punctuation point that ends the episode is reached when a certain aesthetic or sentiment has been experienced in conjoint action. Making a difference, making things "just so," and working until it "feels right" are not fully captured or expressed in the words the members use. Developing an understanding of the Acadian Americans' meaning of working cannot rely solely on words they use. Knowing must include feelings and the aesthetical dimensions the members used to describe their actions. The consummatory aspect of communication provides us with descriptions of how things fit together in "beautiful ways" or create degrees of discomfort. Within this study it has been found that emotions cannot be discounted when explaining the meaning of working. These aesthetical dimensions and consummatory experiences allow a reading of the Acadian Americans' bond to working, and how working has such prominence in their lives. What the members described were emotional experiences that were instrumental in telling them when working was achieving its purpose. For the Acadian Americans this experience tells them that they are living a good life. In the analysis there were statements made referring to the emotions they experienced as necessary. These consummatory moments reaffirm their beliefs about working and what it means to be a person. There were clear indications that the members understood each other when they described these emotional experiences about working. In fact, the reflexive need to extend these emotional accounts about working was very much a part of the interaction in the interviews. The common understanding, and use of the aesthetical in relation to work, revealed the member's emotional adeptness in the interaction. Averill (1980) described emotions as emerging in coherent ways in patterns of social action. He also described these emotional states as transitory, and socially constructed. The social aspects of these experiences were apparent among the Acadian Americans. There was a high degree of coherence among the members, and their description about beautiful moments and awful moments at work had common features they readily understood. The meaning of these felt emotions was intelligible and a substantial feature of an Acadian-American experience of working. This consummatory experience is expressed frequently by the members, and talked about often in relation to the good feeling of a job well done, or the terrible feelings of something not done well. Dewey described communication and living with others in association as not simply instrumental. Communication and life within a community are consummatory as the members' lives are made richer by living in association with moral orders that lead them to a sense of fulfillment which is far greater than what would come about living a life in isolation.[3]

Consummatory experiences provided punctuation points for the members in episodes of interaction. The episode stops when there is communal agreement, and this agreement is known to the members by the feeling of things being right. Consummatory experiences also inform members when their work efforts are right or not right. This form of experience was essential to everyday practices and served as a guiding force in the interaction between members.

The Acadian Americans showed that there are different ways that consummatory experiences may be organized. In their description of the consummatory experiences of working, they talked about an awareness that they were building to it, but it was deeply felt only later in reflection. They did not describe peak experiences until they reach the end of the episode, when they stand back and say this was a good day, or this job was done well. Other people may have peak moments in the doing of the event, and the reflection provides more of a summary statement that the event or episode was beautiful. How consummatory experiences are organized should not be seen as universal and following the same sequence for all people. Aesthetical experiences are contingent upon the social construction of reality and conjoint action of people which create multiple possibilities for experiences.

What Can Be Said about Working

The grammar of working includes a wide array of practices, feelings, rules, and a structure that has been made by people living in action. What has been shown throughout the study is that working for this culture is not a thing or an object, but instead it should be thought of as lived action. The recursive features of communication have shown that working is both created by these actors and then serves as a context for their actions. The consequentiality of communication has led the Acadian Americans to socially construct an understanding of working that is unique to them and represents how they go about living their lives. Their shared perspective of how a life is to be lived has lead them to see work as a central feature of what a person does. This account of working through the process of communication leads to a different understanding of what working is, and provides a different perspective on where to look to understand working.

Work does not lead the Acadian Americans to the good life; it *is* the good life. Through working they develop selfhood, generate community, satisfy moral forces, reaffirm their culture, care for their family, and have a closer relationship to their God. The Acadian American's meaning of working shares some common features with the Encyclical of John Paul II that stressed strong moral obligations (Pope John Paul II, 1981). John Paul II believed family life and social order are made possible through the means of subsistence. While the Acadian

Americans share these moral obligations their story of working is not a story about subjugating nature or transforming the world as John Paul II stressed. Subjugation of nature and transformation of the world are ends, and work is the instrument to achieve them. The Acadian Americans do not work to achieve ends such as these. For them working is what a good person does and it by itself represents the good life. There are cultures that see working as a tool that helps you to get the life you want. Working can lead to ownership of objects, power, status, or satisfaction. The Acadian Americans do not see work as a tool. Working is intrinsic to a way of living and working hard is a good life. Acadian Americans frequently spoke of making the best of a situation. This is not as difficult as it may be for others. The Acadian American is likely to view challenges in the environment as warranting hard work, and working hard is what a person does. A difficult situation is a challenge, but it may be overcome by perseverance and the act of working hard. It is significant to this study that the Acadian Americans do not make distinctions between work at home, at a job, or in the community. They do not make these distinctions because working is what a person does in all aspects of living. The forces to work hard are the same in all aspects of your life.

Thinking of the meaning of working as a conjoint construction tells us that working can take on multiple meanings, each with its own rules and practices, that guide people in the action of working. Through their situated interaction people can construct a different view of what work is and what part it plays in selfhood. The meaning of working does not reside within the interior of a person, nor is it fixed. The making of the meaning of working is not an individual act; its meaning is made in the process of interaction.

This study does not attempt to offer absolute truths about working. A study grounded in CMM has presented arguments that there are no absolute truths to be discovered. A world that is in process of being made cannot rely on static principles or conceptions. Each situation opens new ways of thinking and acting which means working will be different and contextually dependent.

Final Thoughts

As stated several times, the meaning of a term such as *working* is made by people in a given context through the ongoing process of communication. Its direction cannot be predicted, and we cannot expect that other people in other places will construct the same meanings. Meanings, grammars, and actions made in the process of interaction are also affected by the affordances and constraints that are imposed on the environment. The Acadian-American story of working has a long and enduring history that shaped the rules and forces in their world. The Acadian Americans also face a future and a changing environment that present them with new challenges and choices for living. It is likely that their interaction will lead them to construct and adapt their ideas of working in a manner consistent with the structure they have conjointly created.

Infinite possibilities for action exist and this study explored how action is within a group, how it is constructed, how it is reaffirmed, and how at times it is changed. This is one study of one group of people who have constructed a world where work is featured prominently in their lives. This study does not reveal universal principles about working that are true for all people in all places, but it does show the multiple factors and experiences that are woven into the meaning of a prevalent social institution. Hopefully this study will serve as an example of a practical research method capable of examining the structures of grammar people use in situated interaction. The study provided an analysis of the participants' moral orders and logical forces that tell them what should and should not be done in an episode of interaction. This approach allowed an analysis of the recursivity and reflexiveness of communication, and it accounted for the aesthetical dimensions of the experience of working. CMM represented a tool and a method that allowed the researcher to enter into the grammar of the members in order to describe the action and logical forces of ongoing communication. The researcher was able to explore the details of the Acadian Americans' lives evident in communication episodes. This exploration included aesthetical and other nonverbal dimensions which provided a thick description of the meaning of working.

When the focus of research is exploring meaning, as this study does, the researcher must be reminded that meaning exists differently than objects, and researchers imposes their own affects on the data in front of them. The researcher may ask how much can be taken from episodes played out in front of you with a group of people that openly admit they mistrust many people outside of their community. I feel I had an advantage as a researcher among the Acadian Americans having lived within this community for twenty years, and being married to an Acadian American who has maintained strong ties to her family and community. The data was presented in English, but there were times the members would code-switch and use French terms or words. I am not fluent in French, but I am familiar with the dialect, the phrases used, and the expressive tone of the members, which gave me an ability to understand the interactions. My role in this study was not to judge what went on in situated interaction; instead, CMM provided a way to intelligently join in the activity of the Acadian Americans to enrich it or understand it (Cronen, 1994).

CMM is usually concerned with identifying different levels of stories which occur in a hierarchical relationship. In this study the stories the members told did not constitute separate levels, but instead were indicative of an integrated story. For example, many of the stories about religion also served as stories about the Acadian-American community. While the members would use the terms to indicate a story of one kind, it would often be closely related to stories in other areas of their life due to the intertwined nature of the stories. In an instance such as this, the researcher may find that identifying the levels of the stories is not as important as it usually is conceived of in a CMM analysis.

Another consideration for researchers is to recognize that, while a study like this may be read to represent a unified picture, this is not a unified picture of life for Acadian Americans. As was indicated in several sections, there were times when the members felt tensions with the rules for action, or frustration with the "right way" of doing things. CMM does not seek an integrated whole and this analysis showed that this is not a perfect unity. The suggestion is offered to other researchers using the CMM methodology to avoid seeking perfect unities, as people do not live within one totally integrated whole.

Practical Implications

A study about working should have practical value for people faced with the challenges of everyday life. CMM, developed in the tradition of American pragmatist philosophy, has the goal of meliorating challenges and issues in order to improve the life of people living in the world. A practical theory and study of working may offer several directions for managers, leaders, and others grappling with making sense of the term *working*. Foremost is the guiding idea that working is a concept that is constructed within patterns of joint action. Therefore, the primary place to look in order to understand working in an institution is in the communication of people in that context. Those wanting to understand working should explore the ways people work together in an organization. As this study has stated several times, there are no set prescriptions that define working. People acting together construct a grammar of what working is. Therefore, managers and leaders may benefit from acting as inquirers in an evolving, open-ended social world. This would mean that an appreciation needs to be developed for the constitutive nature of communication and the role it plays in creating and sustaining the grammar of working. Managers and leaders can develop abilities to enter into the workers' grammar, which may promote an understanding of what rules, and practices people call upon, and what meanings are informing their actions. They may find benefits in becoming better observers and participants in the interactions around them. Acting as a participant-observer may lead them to rethink and discover the recursive nature of communication, the relationships they are participants in, cultures in the workplace, the meanings people call upon, the forces for action, and the importance of the aesthetical dimensions of working.

There are different contexts of communication in organizational life organized by different rules. People's actions and meanings are apposite to the evolving context of communication. Context refers to the way aspects of behavior such as joint action, punctuation, the setting, and interests are woven together in the process of communication. Not all people within a given context share the same interests, and differences are likely to occur in the contexts where people encounter one another. As was shown in this study, Acadian Americans bring widely different interests to the work setting, which has different consequences for action. These differences may be attributed to the moral action which is part of the characteristics of communication. Moral forces vary across cultures and organizations and these forces tell a person what they can do, must do, must not do, and what degree of responsibility they have within in a particular episode. Managers and leaders may want to think of culture in different ways. In this study Acadian Americans integrated notions of family, culture, working, and church into an almost impermeable bond. Their construction of culture leads one to think culture is not a static list of variables that reduces people to simple lists of beliefs or practices. What this study revealed was that culture is a way of making sense of thought and action and informs a person's abilities and guides action.

Lastly, this study offers managers and leaders evidence that change is a universal condition of life. Change often brings with it disorder, but it also opens new possibilities. This goal of this study was not to promote, or even comment on the ways of acting. The goal was to offer ways of entering into a context and to explore the grammar of people there to find how this contributes to the meaning of the term *working*. In so doing people may find ways to better understand the uniqueness of the contexts of work. Such an appreciation and understanding can lead to better ways of acting,

Future Directions for the Study of Work

The Acadian Americans' grammar of working provide us with a starting point for another way to research the meaning of working. The majority of research completed on the subject of working has not included work in the home or community. The Acadian Americans do not see the action of working as bounded by the distinctions of paid and non-paid work. These non-paid occurrences of work may have important implications that should be explored in understanding the meaning of work. The Acadian Americans also remind us that work does not have an obvious opposing concept called leisure. Even within the stories of leisure, there are strong forces for working and fulfilling obligations to FCWc.

Within the larger frame working appears to be a relatively taken-for-granted concept. However, working is filled with morals, rules, aesthetic dimensions, and a grammar. Through the process of living a grammar of selfhood emerges and as grammars differ so do the conceptions of self and action. This observation may have greater implications for understanding what working means and its impact on community and individuals. While this study concludes without providing foundational truths about working, it suggests that exploring the course of interaction offers important ways to understand the actions and meaning of working.

It is with the utmost sincerity that I offer my thanks to the Acadian Americans who participated in the interviews. While their culture is not one that has drawn much attention among researchers they offer us important concepts to consider as we explore work, culture, and human communication. Their stories and their lives achieve one of their greatest moral goals; they do make a difference.

Notes

Chapter 2

1. The Acadians are briefly introduced here but the reader is directed to *The Acadians of the Maritimes: Thematic Studies.* This work, produced by the Center for Acadian Studies at the University of Moncton (1981), provides a detailed history of the Acadians.
2. Neither the census of the City of Gardner nor that of the Commonwealth of Massachusetts distinguished between Acadian and Québécois. See Massachusetts Department of Commerce and Development (1964, 1973) for 1960 and 1970 census data for the time period this study focuses on.
3. With relatively little formal data available on the Acadians, much of this history is reliant upon oral histories of both the Québécois and the Acadians who came to the mill towns of New England. See the following sources regarding efforts to research the Franco-American experience in New England: Doty & Federal Writers' Project., 1985; Quintal, 1996; Theriault, 1980. Efforts by the Franco-American Institute at Assumption College and by the University of Maine at Fort Kent have been dedicated to collecting the oral histories of Acadian and Québécois people.
4. Interest in the Acadian identity has grown in both the United States and Canada. An Acadian Party was formed in New Brunswick in 1972. The University of Moncton has dedicated a museum and archives to Acadian history. The University of Maine at Fort Kent also maintains an Acadian archive that includes fifteen linear feet of manuscript materials, 8,500 photographic images, 450 audio or video recordings and films, 200 microfilm rolls, 2,000 reference books and journals, 100 maps and other materials on regional history and culture. An Acadian cultural society is located in nearby Fitchburg, Massachusetts, which conducts regular meetings and maintains a website with a variety of resources about Acadian history, genealogy, culture, and announcements of cultural events in the area.

Chapter 3

1. The exact place of Roman Catholicism in the lives of Acadians earlier than the late eighteenth century is vague due to a lack of historical documents verifying how widely Catholicism was practiced, or the number of Acadians who were members of the church. Roman Catholicism had become the predominant religion of the Acadians by the end of the eighteenth century

and continues so to the present day (see Griffiths, 1992). After the return of the Acadians to the Maritimes, Catholic priests were scarce, as English governors placed many restrictions on Acadian life. Villagers would gather for Sunday Mass usually without a priest. It was on rare occasions that a priest would conduct a Mass in the villages. In the early 1800s two visits were made by French-speaking Bishops from Quebec. Shortly after these visits, English authorities ruled that the Acadians were to remain under English-speaking bishops in Fredericton who were either Irish or Scottish. There is evidence of a deliberate action to install English-speaking priests. Without schools to provide training it was not until the early 1900s that the Acadians had priests who could speak their language or were familiar with their culture. The establishment of a classical college in the Maritimes and of a French-speaking bishop in New Brunswick in 1912 changed the availability of priests who were sensitive to the needs of the Acadians (Rose, 1953).

2. A definition and description of these Roman Catholic sacraments are provided in chapter 4. It will also be shown how the members' actions mirror the practices that are found in these sacraments.

3. The Meaning of Work research project investigated the meanings people attach to working within eight industrialized countries (Belgium, Britain, Germany, Israel, Japan, Netherlands, the United States, Yugoslavia). Through the collaborative efforts of several national teams that performed joint comparative research, the project studied more than 14,000 workers.

Chapter 4

1. Many more writers were associated with pragmatism in both its early and more recent period than could be represented here, or are relevant to this study. Readers should keep in mind that the meaning and application of pragmatism are actively being debated. The goal of pragmatism was never to become a philosophy, but to serve as way of thinking or doing philosophy. Pragmatism has avoided becoming a school of thought or a discipline.

2. CMM, like pragmatism, means to improve ways of living. Philosophy and research are raised to arts of living, and in so doing their goal is to make practical, life situations better.

3. The Milan Group consisted of Luigi Boscolo, Mara Selvini Pallazzoli, Gianfranco Cecchin, and Gioulianna Prata, a team of therapists working in Milan. Within their work they focused on levels of meaning which they felt derived from context. Their work led to a method of interviewing called circular questioning. See Tomm (1987) for a history and description of the method.

Chapter 5

1. See Psathas, G. (1995). *Conversation analysis: The study of talk-in-interaction.* Thousand Oaks, CA: Sage Publications, for transcription symbols used in the transcripts presented throughout this study—which, however, are somewhat simplified in this book.

2. See Harney, R. (1982). Franco-Americans and ethnic studies: Notes on a Mill Town, in *The Quebec and Acadian Diaspora in North America,* (Breton, R. & Savard, P., eds.). Here Harney provides a description of the French Canadians as being underrepresented in political jobs, sheltered from the larger community in the city of Salem, Massachusetts, and unnoticed by most groups in the area.

Chapter 6

1. As discussed in chapter 1, the Acadians who returned to the Maritimes after the diaspora lived under restrictions imposed by the English government, which limited the number of

priests and kept control of their churches under English-speaking bishops. These factors may have influenced the making of a different kind of Catholicism.

Chapter 7

1. Data on Acadian Americans who receive public assistance and unemployment benefits are not available. The Commonwealth of Massachusetts does not recognize the Acadians or Acadian Americans as a distinct group. The information about the Acadians and Acadian-Americans' hesitancy to use public assistance services are based upon anecdotal information and my experience with human service agencies in the City of Gardner for approximately fifteen years.

Chapter 11

1. In chapter 5 it was stated that the transcript could not capture the energy and sentiment expressed by the participants. As it was described the members shared a high level of interaction, laughter, and deep conviction during the interviews. The pattern of frequent interruptions and emphasis the participants place on certain words and points in the conversation are important aspects of their communication. This is an Acadian-American way of talking, which has its own rules and feel and is essential to understanding what meanings they bring to interaction.

2. The power of communion in the Acadian Americans' lives is affirmed in their religious beliefs. At a Mass I attended at Notre Dame du Saint Rosaire (Our Lady of the Holy Rosary), a reading for the ceremony was taken from The Gospel of John (14:18 and 16:22) that stated "the Lord said I will not leave you orphans. I will come back to you and your hearts will rejoice Alleluia." The communion they share moves them from a life of isolation to one in which they celebrate community and are never left orphaned.

3. Dewey was actually referring to community life, communication, and living in association. He was discussing the concept of democracy as able to provide for the development of commonality and cooperation. In living with others we have " the power to be an individualized self making a distinctive contribution and enjoying in its own way the fruits of association" (*Later Works* 2:329).

Bibliography

Averill, J. (1980). A constructivist view of emotion. In Plutchik, R. K. & Kellerman, H. (Eds.), *Theories of Emotion*. New York: Academic Press.

Barker, R. (1968). *Ecological Psychology*. Palo Alto, CA: Stanford University Press

Bateson, G. (1972). *Steps to an Ecology of Mind: Collected Essays in Anthropology, Psychiatry, Evolution, and Epistemology*. San Francisco: Chandler Pub. Co.

Boydston, J. A. (1970). *Guide to the Works of John Dewey*. Carbondale: Southern Illinois University Press.

Broderick, R. (1987). *The Catholic Encyclopedia*. Nashville: T. Nelson Publishing.

Brookes, A. (1976). Out-migration from the Maritime provinces 1860–1900: Some preliminary considerations. *Acadiens* (Spring 1976), p.28.

Buzzanell, P. (1994). Gaining a voice: Feminist organizational communication theorizing. *Management Communication Quarterly* 7, 339–383.

Center for Acadian Studies (1981). *The Acadians of the Maritimes: Thematic Studies.* Moncton, NB: University of Moncton.

Changsheng, X. (1991). Communication in China: A case study of Chinese collectivist and self interest talk in social action from the CMM perspective. Unpublished Ph.D. thesis, University of Massachusetts, Amherst.

Cheney, G. (1995). Democracy in the workplace: Theory and practice from the perspective of communication. *Journal of Applied Communication Research* 23, 167–200.

Choquette, L. (2000). Director of The Franco-American Institute, Assumption College. Personal communication regarding data collected on Acadians in America (March15).

Clark, A. (1988). Coming to America. *Gardner Today,* October 19.

Cronen, V. (1991). Coordinated Management of Meaning Theory and Post-Enlightenment Ethics. In Greenberg, K. J. (Ed.), *Conversations on Communication Ethics*. Norwood, NJ: Ablex.

———— (1994). Coordinated management of meaning: Theory for the complexities and contradictions of everyday life. In Siegfried, J. (Ed.), *The Status of Common Sense in Psychology*. Norwood, NJ: Ablex.

———— (1995a). Coordinated Management of Meaning: The Consequentiality of Communication and the Recapturing of Experience. In Sigman, S. J. (Ed.), *The Consequentiality of Communication*. Hillsdale, NJ: Lawrence Erlbaum.

———— (1995b). Coordinated management of meaning: Practical theory and the tasks ahead for social approaches to communication. In Leeds-Hurwitz, W. (Ed.), *Social Approaches to Communication*. New York: Guilford Press.

———— (2000a). Practical theory and a naturalistic account of inquiry. Unpublished paper at the conference on practical theory, public participation, and community. Baylor University, Waco, TX.

———— (2000b). Education as teaching inquiry: Practical art and theory in the pragmatic tradition. Paper presented at the National Communication Association annual meeting, Seattle.

———— (2000c) Lecture on CMM. Kennsington Consultation Centre Oxford Summer workshop (July 4). Bristol, UK.

Cronen, V., Chen, V. & Pearce, W. B. (1988). Coordinated management of meaning: A critical theory. In Gudykunst, K.Y. & W. (Eds.), *Theories in Intercultural Communication*. Beverly Hills: Sage.

Cronen, V. & Chetro-Szivos, J. (2001). Pragmatism as a way of inquiring with special reference to a theory of communication and the general form of pragmatic social theory. In Perry, D. (Ed.), *Pragmatism and Communication Research*. Highland, MD: Erlbaum.

Cronen, V., & Lang, P. (1994). Language and action: Wittgenstein and Dewey in the practice of therapy and consultation. *Human Systems: The Journal of Systemic and Consultation and Management* 5, 5–43.

Cronen, V., Pearce, B., & Xi, C. (1989). The meaning of meaning. *Research on Language and Social Interaction* 23, 1–40.

Daigle, J. (1982). The Acadians: A people in search of a country. In Breton, R. & Savard, P. (Eds.), *The Quebec and Acadian Diaspora in North America*. Toronto: Multicultural History Society of Ontario.

Deetz, S. (1982). Critical interpretive research in organizational communication. *The Western Journal of Speech Communication* 46, 131–149.

Dewey, J. (1916). *Democracy and Education: An Introduction to the Philosophy of Education*. New York: Macmillan.

———— (1920/1948). *Reconstruction in Philosophy*. Enlarged edition. New York: The Free Press.

———— (1922). *Human Nature and Conduct*. New York: Holt.

———— (1925). *Experience and Nature*. Chicago, London: Open Court Publishing Company.

———— (1931). *Philosophy and Civilization*. New York: Minton Press.

———— (1934). *Art as Experience*. New York: Minton Balch & Company.

———— (1938). *Logic: The Theory of Inquiry*. New York: Holt and Company.

———— (1967). *The Early Works, 1882–1898*. Carbondale: Southern Illinois University Press.

———— (1976) *The Middle Works, 1899–1924*. Carbondale: Southern Illinois University Press.

———— (1981). *The Later Works, 1925–1953*. Carbondale: Southern Illinois University Press.

Doty, C. S. & Federal Writers' Project. (1985). *The First Franco-Americans: New England Life Histories from the Federal Writers' Project, 1938–1939* (1st ed.). Orono: University of Maine Press.

Dubin, R. (1956). Industrial workers' worlds: A study of the "central life interests" of industrial workers. *Social Problems* 3, 131–142.

Epstein, C. F. (1990). The cultural perspective and the study of work. In Erickson, K.T. & Vallas, S. P. (Eds.), *The nature of work* (p. 378). New Haven: Yale University Press.

Fishman, J. (1981). Language maintenance and ethnicity. *Canadian Review of Studies in Nationalism* VIII:2 (Fall 1981), 233–34.

Foley, P. (1999). Paradox and promise in the dialogue on race: A case study analysis of the dialogues of the Springfield (MA) World Class City Commission. Unpublished doctoral dissertation, The University of Massachusetts, Amherst.

Fryer, D. (1931). *The measurement of Interests in Relation to Human Adjustment*. Troy, MO: Holt, Rinehart & Winston.

Geertz, C. (1973). *The Interpretation of Cultures*. New York: Basic Books.

Gergen, K. (1973). Social psychology as history. *Journal of Personality and Social Psychology* 26, 309–320.

Gouinlock, J. (1972). *John Dewey's Philosophy of Value*. New York: Humanities Press.

Griffiths, N. (1973). *The Acadians: Creation of a People*. Montreal: McGraw-Hill.

———— (1992). *The Contexts of Acadian History, 1686–1784*. Montreal, Buffalo: Published for the Centre for Canadian Studies, Mount Allison University by McGill-Queen's University Press.

Habermas, J. (1984). *The Theory of Communicative Action*. Boston: Beacon Press.

Hall, B. (1992). Theories of culture and communication. *Communication Theory* 2, 50–70.

Harney, R. (1982). Franco-Americans and ethnic studies: Notes on a mill town. In Breton, R. & Savard, P. (Eds.), *The Quebec and Acadian Diaspora in North America* (pp. xix, 199). Toronto: Multicultural History Society of Ontario.

Haslett, B. J., Geis, F. L. & Carter, M. (1992). *The Organizational Woman: Power and Paradox*. Norwood, NJ: Ablex.

Hegel, G. (1975) (Knox, T.M., Trans.). *Lectures on Aesthetics* (Vol.1). Oxford: Clarendon Press.

Heider, F. (1958). *The Psychology of Interpersonal Relations*. New York: Wiley.

James, W. (1907). *Pragmatism, A New Name for Some Old Ways of Thinking: Popular Lectures on Philosophy*. New York: Longmans Green and Co.

———— (1909). *A Pluralistic Universe: Hibbert Lectures to Manchester College on the Present Situation in Philosophy*. New York: Longmans Green and Co.

James, W. & Perry, R. B. (1912). *Essays in Radical Empiricism*. New York: Longmans Green and Co.

Pope John Paul II. (1981). Encyclical: *Laborem exercens*. Vatican City, September 14.

Kanungo, R. (1979). The concept of alienation and involvement revisited. *Psychological Bulletin* 56, 119–138.

———— (1982). Measurement of job and work involvement. *Journal of Applied Psychology* 67, 341–349.

Kimeldorf, H. (1985). Working class culture, occupational recruitment and union politics. *Social Forces* 64 (2).

Kvale, S. (1996). *Interviews: An Introduction to Qualitative Research Interviewing*. Thousand Oaks, CA: Sage Publications.

Lamphere, L. (1985). Bringing the family to work: Women's culture on the shop floor. *Feminist Studies* 11, 519–540.

Lawler, E. E. & Hall, D. T. (1970). Relationship of job characteristics to job involvement, satisfaction, and intrinsic motivation. *Journal of Applied Psychology* 54, 305–312.

Leeds-Hurwitz, W. (1995). Introducing social approaches. In Leeds-Hurwitz, W. (Ed.), *Social Approaches to Communication*. New York: Guilford Press.

Lodahl, T. & Kejner, M. (1965). The definition and measurement of job involvement, satisfaction, and intrinsic motivation. *Journal of Applied Psychology* 49, 24–33.

Malloy, T. (1984). *Profiles of the Past: An Illustrated History of Ashburnham, Gardner, Hubbardston, Templeton, Westminster, and Winchendon, Massachusetts*. Athol, MA: Millers River Publishing Co.

Mead, G. H. & Morris, C. W. (1934). *Mind, Self and Society From the Standpoint of a Social Behaviorist*. Chicago: The University of Chicago Press.

Moore, E. (1967). *History of Gardner Massachusetts 1785–1967*. Gardner, MA: Hatton Printing Inc.

MOW International Research Team. (1987). *The Meaning of Working.* London, Orlando, FL.: Academic Press.

Mumby, D. (1988*). Communication and Power in Organizations: Discourse, Ideology, and Domination.* Norwood, NJ: Ablex.

———— (1992). The politics of emotion: A feminist reading of bounded rationality. *Academy of Management Review* 17, 465–486.

Mumby, D. and. Stohl., C. (1996). Disciplining organizational communication studies. *Management Communication Quarterly* 10 (August 1996 Issue 1), 50–83.

Ortner, S. (1974). Is female to male as nature is to culture? In Rosaldo, M. Z. & Lamphere, L. (Eds.), *Women, Culture and Society.* Cambridge: Cambridge University Press.

Pearce, W. B. (1989). *Communication and the Human Condition.* Carbondale: Southern Illinois University Press.

———— (1994). *Interpersonal Communication: Making Social Worlds.* New York: HarperCollins.

Pearce, W. B. & Cronen, V. (1980). *Communication, Action, and Meaning: The Creation of Social Realities.* New York: Praeger.

Peirce, C. (1905). What pragmatism is. *The Monist* XV, 161–181.

Peirce, C. S. & Buchler, J. (1940). *The Philosophy of Peirce: Selected Writings.* New York, London: Harcourt Brace; K. Paul Trench Trubner & Co. Ltd.

Peirce, C. S., Hartshorne, C. & Weiss, P. (1931). *Collected Papers of Charles Sanders Peirce.* Cambridge: Belknap Press of Harvard University Press.

Psathas, G. (1995). *Conversation Analysis: The Study of Talk-in-Interaction.* Thousand Oaks. CA: Sage Publications.

Putnam, H. (1995). *Pragmatism: An Open Question.* Oxford: Blackwell.

Quintal, C. (1996). *Steeples and Smokestacks: A Collection of Essays on the Franco-American Experience in New England. Worcester, MA:* Assumption College Institut Français.

Rabinowitz, S. & Hall, D. T. (1977). Organizational research on job involvement. *Psychological Bulletin* 84, 265–288.

Remy, L. (1910). *The Catholic Encyclopedia* (Vol. VIII). New York: Appleton Press.

Rorty, R. (1979). *Philosophy and the Mirror of Nature.* Princeton, NJ: Princeton University Press.

Rose, D. (1953). The Franco-Americans of Gardner: A study in immigration. Unpublished thesis, Harvard University, Cambridge, MA.

Rus, V. and Arezensek, V. (1984). *Work as Destiny and Liberty: Division and Alienation of Work.* Zagreb: Liber.

Saleh, S. D. (1981). A structural view of job involvement and its differentiation from satisfaction and motivation. *International Review of Applied Psychology*, 30, 17–30.

Seeman, M. (1959). On the meaning of alienation. *American Sociological Review,* 24, 783–791.

Shotter, J. (1984). *Social Accountability and Selfhood.* Oxford: Basil Blackwell.

Shusterman, R. (1997). *Practicing philosophy: Pragmatism and the Philosophical Life.* New York: Routledge.

Stinchcombe, A. (1990). Work institutions and the sociology of everyday life. In Erickson, K. T. & Vallas, S. P. (Eds.), *The Nature of Work.* New Haven, CT: Yale University Press.

Strong, E. (1943). *The Vocational Interests of Men and Women.* Palo Alto, CA: Stanford University Press.

Super, D. (1980). A Life-span, life-space, approach to career development. *Journal of Vocational Behavior* 16, 282–298.

———— (1995). Values: Their nature, assessment and practical use. In Super, D. (Ed.), *Life, Roles, Values and Careers: International Findings of the Work Importance Study.* San Francisco: Jossey-Bass.

Sverko, B. and. Vizek-Vidovick., V. (1995). Studies of the meaning of work: Approaches, models, and some of the findings. In Super, D. (Ed.), *Life Roles, Values, and Careers: International Findings of the Work Importance Study* (3–21). San Francisco: Jossey-Bass.

Tannen, D. (1990). *You Just Don't Understand: Women and Men in Conversation*. New York: William Morrow and Company.

Thayer, H. S. (1968). *Meaning and Action: A Critical History of Pragmatism*. Indianapolis: Bobbs–Merrill Co.

Theriault, G. F. (1980). *The Franco-Americans in a New England Community: An Experiment in Survival*. New York: Arno Press.

Tilgher, A. (1962). Work: What it has meant to men through the ages. In Nosov, S. and Form, W. H. (Eds.), *Man, Work, and Society*. New York: Basic Books.

Tomm, K. (1987). One perspective on the Milan systemic approach. *Family Process* 26, 38–63.

——— (1988). Interventive interviewing: Part III, Intending to ask lineal, circular, strategic, or reflexive questions. *Family Process* 27, 1–15.

Volosinov, V. (1976/1927). *Freudianism: A Critical Sketch*. Bloomington: Indiana University Press.

Warriner, C. (1970). *The Emergence of Society*. Homewood, IL. Dorsey Press.

Weber, M. (T. Parsons, Trans.) (1958). *The Protestant Ethic and the Spirit of Capitalism*. New York: Scribner.

Weinstein, E. A. and Deutschberger, P. (1963). Some dimensions of altercasting. *Sociometry* 26, 454–466.

Westwood, S. (1982). *All Day, Every Day: Factory and Family in the Making of Women's Lives*. Chicago: University of Illinois Press.

Wilensky, H. L. (1981). Family cycle, work and the quality of life: Reflections on the roots of happiness, despair, and indifference in modern society. In Gardell, B. & Johannson, G. (Eds.), *Working Life*. New York: Wiley.

Wittgenstein, L. (1958). *Philosophical Investigations* (2d ed.). Oxford: Blackwell.

——— (1969). *On Certainty*. Oxford: Basil Blackwell.

Wood, J. (1994). *Gendered Lives: Communication, Gender, and Culture*. Belmont, CA: Wadsworth Publishing Company.

Zuboff, S. (1983). The work ethic and work organization. In Barbash, J. (Ed.), *The Work Ethic: A Critical Analysis*. Madison, WS: Industrial Relations Research Association.

Index

Printed in the United States
59862LVS00008B/18